100 TRICKS EVERY

D0447351

# 100 TRICKS EVERY BOY CAN DO

## HOW MY BROTHER DISAPPEARED

Kim Stafford

**TRINITY UNIVERSITY PRESS**
SAN ANTONIO

Published by Trinity University Press
San Antonio, Texas 78212

Cover design by Rebecca Lown
Book design by BookMatters, Berkeley
Jacket photo courtesy of Anthony Goicolea © 2010

Trinity University Press strives to produce its books using
methods and materials in an environmentally sensitive
manner. We favor working with manufacturers that
practice sustainable management of all natural resources,
produce paper using recycled stock, and manage forests
with the best possible practices for people, biodiversity, and
sustainability. The press is a member of the Green Press
Initiative, a nonprofit program dedicated to supporting
publishers in their efforts to reduce their impacts on
endangered forests, climate change, and forest-dependent
communities.

The paper used in this publication meets the minimum
requirements of the American National Standard for
Information Sciences—Permanence of Paper for Printed
Library Materials, ANSI 39.48–1992.

Library of Congress Cataloging-in-Publication Data

Stafford, Kim Robert.
    100 tricks every boy can do : a memoir / Kim Stafford.
       p.   cm.
    ISBN 978-1-59534-136-5 (pbk.)
    I. Stafford, Kim Robert. 2. Stafford, Bret, 1948–1988.
3. Brothers—Oregon—Biography. 4. Authors, American—
20th century—Biography. I. Title. II. Title: One hundred
tricks every boy can do.
PS3569.T23A3   2012
818.5403—dc23                          2012019210

16   15   14   13   12  |  5   4   3   2   1

Why tell what hurts?

—WILLIAM STAFFORD

# CONTENTS

## III. HAVE SWEET DREAMS

## IV. SEE YOU TOMORROW

# PROLOGUE: THE TRICK

In 1958, when he was ten, my older brother Bret found an ad in the back of a comic book and ordered 100 *Tricks Every Boy Can Do*. When this pamphlet of secrets arrived, he flipped through to the last and most difficult trick: how to jerk a tablecloth away but leave a wine glass standing. Like many tricks in this life, the materials were ordinary, but the required sleight of hand approached the impossible.

He waited until everyone was gone from home, set the Finnish sherry glass on the dishtowel—a handmade crystal that family friends had brought us from afar. Bret held the selvage in his hands, took a breath, and yanked the cloth. Shattered glass flew everywhere.

Long after Bret was gone, I would tell our son, Guthrie, who had never met his uncle, stories of that era when I had a brother and the world was young. It was an era spangled with mysteries and delights.

One day, when Guthrie was ten, as we sat at our family table, he took the edge of the tablecloth in his hands, cast a sly smile in my direction, and said, "Dad, shall I do the trick?"

He laughed, made a feint to twitch the cloth in his hands, and my mind went far. The present moment dropped away, and I watched my brother in a parade of enigmatic moments from childhood through our years together and beyond.

"Guthrie," I said, "I could write a book about Uncle Bret called 100 *Tricks Every Boy Can Do*, and tell all kinds of stories from his life."

"Yeah, Dad," Guthrie said, "but suicide was the trick that didn't work."

Well, one of the tricks that didn't work. In my brother's life, his last desperate day was but one in an array of mysteries. How many tricks are required to become a man? What have been my own encounters with this fierce set of hidden tests and amazing feats? And Guthrie, this man-child in my life—what moments from his story best reveal our need? The essential code must include the tricks of confidence, loneliness, sex, fear, anger— how to begin a courtship and know it is right, how to end a job when it goes wrong, how to crawl from the wreckage when this life falters, how to plunge to the cellar of sorrow and grope for the ladder that might bring you back into some kind of light, no matter how dim or strange.

How many lessons must be clawed from trouble in order to survive? By what infinite practice in sleight of hand does one become a human being?

# BOOK I. GOOD NIGHT

# "EVERY NIGHT WHEN WE WERE SMALL . . ."

My brother was born in the summer of 1948, in August, shortly after Hiroshima Day, three years beyond the war. Our mother went to see the doctor after baby Bret had arrived.

"How are you doing?" the doctor said.

"How soon can I have another?" our mother replied, deflecting concern for herself or her child. She was ebullient, looking forward, far beyond the infant at her side.

So, the next year, in October, I was born, and the golden time began. My birth announcement is written as if by my brother:

> A fine thing! I now have to
> share my bottle with a Kim.
>
> —Bret Stafford

The young couple, Bill and Dorothy, had their two boys, and we were off.

My brother and I were pals, caught snakes, built forts, tried hard to fit the family pantheon of right behavior, and wavered in our glory. Once I had to leave the dinner table for some forgotten infraction. Bret looked down at me, playing gamely alone on the floor.

"We could give Kimmie this old piece of cheese," he suggested, seeking a reprieve for his pal. So I got to return to the table, was handed a plate with the old piece of cheese. I said my own quick Amen over it, and then fell to.

Our friends could not believe we never fought, but it was so. Mornings, we greeted each other across the narrow space between our beds. Evenings, as we huddled side by side on the couch, our parents read to us from a book called *Fifty Famous Stories*. In those tales, King Alfred made a plan to save the kingdom . . . the Black Douglas climbed a ladder to frighten a mother and child . . . the Wise Men of Gotham mocked their King . . . Dick Whittington gave his cat to the Merchant and thus became Lord Mayor of London . . . and Genghis Khan killed his favorite falcon in a rage. Story by story, we were schooled to survive by learning the mysterious ways of the human. Apparently, there were many tricks required to get it right— sometimes you had to be angry, or thoughtful, humble, tender, wise—or foolish—but always brave. These lessons went into our minds like seeds, and we were sent to bed to dream.

Our mother taught third grade. She was a genius at this, despite having the use of only her left arm, from childhood injuries; she kept her right tucked in her pocket, and no one seemed to pay any attention, as she had a graceful, inviting manner. Our father wrote poems, and worked at his college. He was ambitious about his poetry, and later won the National Book Award, but he did his writing before we were awake. When we were small, writing seemed his hobby.

A sister, Kit, came to us, then another, Barbara. We six were a tribe that moved to a new land every year—Oregon, Iowa, Oregon, Indiana, California, Oregon. It seems our parents kept trying out the Midwest again, where they had been born, or searching always for the better job. I don't remember questioning; in spring, as if we were wild birds, it was time to leave everything behind, and travel far away.

I thought my powers of understanding and confidence (and humbled foolishness) were my brother's powers as well. Days were serene.

When Bret was nine, in January of 1958, back in Oregon, he told our father he was writing a story: "The Mystery of a Gun. This gun, when it shoots, says a word—the sound of the owner's name." Our father wrote this little story down in his notebook, and saved it for later.

A gun that would say your name? Where did that come from?

Our lives were idyllic in many ways. We camped, hiked through deserts and mountains, made forts in the woods near our house, where we could wander in safety in those days.

And every night when we were small, just before sleep my brother would whisper from his bed, "Shall we make a bridge?" I would slide out with my hands walking to his side, my feet propped on my bed, and he would crawl across my back to my bed, and then he would make a bridge, and I would crawl across him to mine, and then from our two beds we would hum and sing and babble until our words began to grow soft with sleep, and then I would hear his voice chant our blessing poem—

> Good night,
> God bless you,
> Have sweet dreams,
> See you tomorrow . . .

because we had developed this way to guard the day's end, and I would reply to him softly enough so our parents would not hear from the living room down the hall, but he could hear me well, just there, "Good night, God bless you, have sweet dreams, see you tomorrow," and then the understanding was that nothing more could be said, or need be said, for we had covered the bases of farewell, blessing, gift, and hope, and so could sleep, and we did. And then we woke up and it was high school, but still, somehow, as if to keep one landmark firm in a storm of change from his bed, through the soft Oregon dark just shadowed by Douglas fir limbs across the streetlight outside, from across the room I would hear, "Good night, God bless you, have sweet dreams, see you tomorrow," and I would reply in kind, and then there were years and he was gone—to college, and into mystery, and we went our separate ways, to towns apart, to jobs, to families of our own, but still by dark so soft I will disturb no one—not wife or child—but addressing the soft Oregon dark I whisper to him, and then I listen . . . listen . . . in the dark I listen for my brother.

## NO GIFT

Christmas Eve, 1987, as we threw our presents into a box for the drive to my sister's house for the big family gathering, I realized I had a gift for everyone but my brother. My wife, Beverly, and our daughter, Rosie, yes. My sisters, Kit and Barb, yes. Mother and Daddy, yes. My brother's wife, Lynne, and their daughter, Katie, and son, Matt, all yes. But my brother, no. In haste, I scrawled on a card, "Bret—let's have lunch together once a month in the coming year. —your brother, Kim."

In the frenzy that night, across the room, I watched my brother. He was a slight man, shorter and thinner than me, though a year older. Dressed in a plaid shirt, observing everyone from a chair just out of the lamplight. His mouth, as often, slightly open, showing his shy smile. His gray eyes shone, the lids slightly lowered, as if he had decided he could not afford to be surprised by anything. He was holding on. Any change in his resolve would hurt too much.

Now I see these details in his face. Then I did not. He was just my brother, and he carried with him, I thought, a lifetime of joys we had shared. I projected over his sorrow the light of our early days, and by this I was blind to him.

When the time came that night, Bret opened my card, read it, glanced at me, and nodded. We had a plan.

Though we lived in the same state, we had not seen each other much. I was teaching at Lewis & Clark College, in Portland, where our father had taught, and had just published a book of essays called *Having Everything Right*. He had been working as a land-use planner in Hood River, an hour east of Portland. That was just far enough to keep us from meeting by whim, as we had in earlier days. And then he had moved his family—wife Lynne, daughter Katie, and son Matthew—to Salem, an hour south from me. But before parting that night we agreed on a day to meet for lunch in Aurora, a little town between us.

He drove north from his job at the Marion County Planning Department, and I drove south from Lewis & Clark. We met at a tavern bordered on both sides by antique stores, ordered hamburgers and beer. The small-town lunch crowd was talkative, and we seemed to fit in—two brothers catching up on family and work. We skated the surface that day, but ended with a plan to meet the next month in Donald, a little farm town west of the freeway between Portland and Salem.

This time my brother rode his bike—a good twenty miles through the farmland he was sworn to protect in his role as county planner. While I waited at the Donald Cafe, I studied the collection of ancient toasters on display—all kinds of mechanisms for the electric transformation of bread, involving sheets of mica, knobs for flipping a slice. And then there came my brother, swinging off the seat and coasting the last half block expertly balanced on the left pedal. We ordered eggs and toast, I told about how my wife, Beverly, had a new wooden flute, and she was working her way through Bach all over again with the softer, more authentic sound. I reported how our daughter, Rosemary, had stopped me at the door the night before, as I departed for a meeting at the college, saying, "Papa, are you a visitor?" "No, I'm not a visitor." Her face brightened: "Then are you staying here tonight?" "No, I have to go to a meeting."

We spoke of meetings, deadlines, of documents.

"I work for the future," Bret said. "Years ago, running water was a luxury. Now everyone considers it a right. But now wise planning is considered a luxury—people don't think they should have to pay for it, deal with it, obey it. I work for a generation beyond us—and they can't help me." He seemed to view his life as a holding action, being brave under siege. Then he looked at his watch, said he would have to bike hard and fast to make it to a meeting. He declined my offer of a ride. We agreed on Lacey's Tavern in Lake Oswego for the next month, and he was off.

Lake Oswego was the town where we grew up, from 1957 onward. We rode our bikes everywhere, collecting enough bottles to cash in for a root beer float whenever we felt like it. We fished the lake and the river, built forts in the woods, terrorized the library, shot bows and arrows into the bank of the school yard, ran a paper route. We generally owned the town as only children in a small place could.

But Lacey's Tavern, at First and B, was a place we had never been.

Bret got there early, and I had to grope my way to the back booth to find him. I was amazed that our hometown had this man den where people seemed to be hiding from daylight—TV over the bar belting out some big game, the eyes of the regulars glinting from their booths. When I turned to my brother, even in the dark, he seemed different, smaller somehow, backed into a corner. We ordered beer to start, and I held up my bottle for a toast, but he didn't move. He didn't sip. I tried to start in on some scrap of news from my life, but he sat still. When I finally recognized this and paused in my rush, he said, "I want my ashes scattered on Mount Adams. . . ." A knife of ice cut my heart. I grabbed my brother's hand, tears in my eyes.

"What are you saying?"

". . . that way, with the water cycle . . ." His voice trailed off. His hand in my hand was cold. I gripped him. He did not grip back.

I could not get more from him. He seemed far away, living a story he did not tell. What had happened? There seemed to be some kind of plan, but he wasn't giving it to me. By prying, I got a few details from him about surface things. Had something big happened in his work? At home? Some fright, or severe defeat? He seemed to be staring something in the face that stunned him. It seemed like an invasion, even an accusation, to demand that my brother tell me. I did not know how to find the deeper place.

Later that month, I went to visit Bret in Salem, with my wife and daughter. Rosie played with Katie and Matt down the hall, and Bret and Lynne offered Beverly and me dessert, and news of their Quaker meeting, a hike they were planning. I studied my brother's face, turned slightly up as was his habit, trying to see if his troubles were visible. He did not return my look, but followed the conversation Lynne was leading about their activities. We passed the evening, and then drove home to Portland.

My ignorance of my brother's life, and of my own, was boundless. In four months my marriage of eighteen years would be over, but I didn't know that. I was a good person, wasn't I? Divorce was impossible. I would last. Maybe my brother was keeping some equivalent half-known endgame from his little brother. He would not say. And I did not share my qualms with him. We seemed to keep a code, protecting each other from knowing what we ourselves barely knew but could feel, like a chill coming from the cave of the future.

What had happened between our second and third meeting? Was Bret about to lose his job? Had something catastrophic happened in his marriage? Did he have a secret about his health, a sudden sense of mortality? Maybe he would tell me when we met again.

I drove down to Boon's Tavern in Salem, and Bret walked from the Marion County office building. He ordered water, and a salad. I had a burger and a beer. This was Salem's historic tavern, where legislators met and deals were struck. It felt like a club of some kind, all dark wood and banter. In our back booth, I began about recent doings. There is so much to say when you think a busy life is what you are supposed to be doing. But eventually, I realized Bret wasn't returning my stories of busy valor with equivalent stories of his own. Finally, he spoke.

"Let me show you something." He opened his wallet, and took out a Chinese cookie fortune. It had been unfolded many times, was gray with wear: "Learn to cut your expectations in half." I felt the knife of ice again.

"No!" I said. "Double your expectations! You have to go for more."

"I can't," he said. "This is how it is. You know how Daddy says about writing, 'Lower your standards and keep going'? That's how I have to do my life."

"Well, what?" I said. "What's so bad?"

"Well," he said, "sometimes at home, at dinner, the only sound is the clink of the silverware."

"I know about that," I said. "We have silences at my house, too. We are raising a child in a world where adults don't laugh, don't touch, don't look at each other." He was still, looking into my eyes. "We have to do something," I said. "We have to."

"I can't," he said again. "We're moving to Canada."

"What?"

"At the end of the summer. I've quit my job. We're selling the house. Lynne has a job teaching in Smithers, B.C. It's about four hundred miles north of the border."

"You're going—that soon?"

"She has wanted to get back to Canada. Her job makes $30,000 . . . plus."

"Bret," I said, "are you sure this is a good idea? You don't have to do this."

"You said so yourself." He glanced into my eyes then looked away. "It says in your book, 'Part of our love must be to teach each other how to live alone.' I need to learn to live away from the family—be on my own."

"That's just a book," I said. "It's not about you. You don't have to go that far."

"But I do," he said. And he stood to return to work.

Our last monthly rendezvous was in the town of Rhododendron on the west slope of Mount Hood. We met in the parking lot at the store, left my car there, and headed east in his, turned off the highway at a road he knew, and followed a gravel track to White River and a glacial outwash plain on the dry east slope. The stream ran milky with glacial polish, and we parked near a grove of wind-shaped trees. It threatened rain, but we got the tent up before the storm hit.

Over a dinner of granola bars and apples, and gritty water from the river, we recalled our camping days—Mount Jefferson, hiking the Skyline Trail, Cove Palisades, Steens Mountain, French Pete.

Then the rain began, and we hunkered down in our sleeping bags in the dark. There was more to say, but we were silent awhile.

"Remember what we used to say?" my brother asked.

"Good night," I said. "God bless you, have sweet dreams, see you tomorrow."

Rain and wind made a symphony over the tent, in the trees, and the river hushed along in the dark.

## "WOULD IT MAKE YOU SAD?"

The first time I met my future father-in-law, when I was nineteen, I wore a red bandana around my neck, a white shirt and white Levis, and no shoes. I came running from the Art Department at the University of Oregon toward my redheaded girl where she balanced and bobbed like a flower beside her father.

"Hello, Dr. Beech," I said, careening to a stop.

"Why, hello," he said, looking me over.

The next day, she told me his assessment: "Kim will never last."

"Is that so?" I thought to myself. "We'll see about that."

Dr. Beech went back to California, and I took my girl to a dance at the Village Green half an hour south of Eugene. When I picked her up in the army-green VW bug I owned with my brother, she climbed in and her seat fell over backward.

"Whoops," I said. "Sorry. I guess the bolts finally rusted out." We got her upright, and we were off.

In June, my brother told me he had read someone's advice about how to keep your girlfriend over the summer.

"Say something that implies a future, without actually proposing," he told me. "Like—'If we ever got a house together, would you want to have a garden?' Or, 'Do you ever think about having kids?' See how that works? It's like half a promise."

I delivered a version of this half-promise while Beverly and I were camped on a narrow ledge in the forest up Eagle Creek in the Columbia Gorge.

"If we ever lived together," I said, "I could be a professor, and you could be an artist." She laughed, I thought in agreement, and that was that.

With this possible future on the table, I departed to hitchhike three months in Europe. I sent her long accounts on thin blue aerograms. "Write me care of American Express," I would say in a carefully printed P.S. after my scrawled stories—"in London . . . in Copenhagen . . . in Göteborg. . . ."

When a letter from her finally reached me in München, I tore it open and read, scanned, delved for love. It was all simple news of daily life. But I was loyal. She must be the one, and her father was wrong.

When Dr. Beech got cancer, I went to Fresno where the family was gathered, to see him. From his hospital bed, he reached out to shake hands.

"You see me as a shell of my former self," he said.

Later that winter, Dr. Beech dwindled and died. But I was loyal. When my girl dropped out of school to live at home, in Fresno, I wrote long letters and was true. And so, in time, we married.

For our honeymoon we hiked up Separation Creek in the Oregon Cascades, carrying Shakespeare's complete works for me, and a spindle and bag of wool for her. In my pack, I had a bottle of red wine, a wedge of cheese, and a giant zucchini we gnawed at half-heartedly. I caught trout and we gathered berries. She sat on a fallen cedar log and drew out a thread from a ball of roving, her spindle whirling in the sun. The air was pungent with pine and affection. Each night she said she felt the spirits all around us. I didn't quite know what that meant, but it sounded right.

We lived in an apartment where the street address included a "½." I gleaned cherries and pears in an old orchard near the river, and she sold her weavings here and there. The first few years, we took turns working. She filled in at the yarn shop while I studied for my degree. Then I was a busboy while she did her weaving, painting, her study to be a librarian. We had books and a loom, and in the evenings there was no TV, just the quiet hum of my reading and thump of the beater as she wove blankets, scarves, and tapestries.

And through it all, as we watched our friends drift apart, find new lives, turn from one love to another, I took pride in our certainty. We were old-fashioned, like our parents. I asked our father once, when he was in a rough patch with our mother, why they stayed together.

"It's the way of my generation," he said. "And there are good times, too."

After twenty years of this loyalty, shortly after meeting my brother at White River, I was driving our daughter, Rosie, age six, to school. She sat on her car seat in the back, as I gripped the wheel and worked my way slowly down the rutted dead-end road where we lived.

"Would it make you sad," she said, "if my mom had to get a new step-husband? Because it seems like she needs one."

"What?" I said.

"That's just my idea about it," she said. I looked in the rearview mirror and met the fierce eyes of our little one.

That night I told my wife what Rosie had said.

"That's funny," Beverly said. "She told me the same thing: 'What if Dad has to get a new step-wife? He seems so sad all the time.'"

"What's that about?" I said.

"This is just the way it is," Beverly said. "This is adult life. It's not all easy."

I guessed she was right. But clearly, loyalty was killing us. Finally I got up the gumption to tell her I had gone to seek counsel from the campus chaplain at the college where I taught and she worked in the library.

"He thinks we should take a trip together," I said. "Leave everything else behind, and just go somewhere beautiful and see what there is for us."

"You shouldn't have talked to him," she said. "I work there, too, you know. He could tell people."

## BROKEN TOP

That summer, a few months after meeting at White River with my brother, I went with my brother-in-law, Steve, and Bret to camp at the foot of Broken Top, the shattered volcanic peak east of the Three Sisters in the Cascade Range. We hiked in at evening, and the meadow at the foot of the mountain was vivid with lupine, paintbrush, sky-blue penstemon. There were so many flowers, it was hard to find a place to pitch our three tents without crushing them. We built a fire, and I was about to add more wood when Bret said, "Remember the old saying: 'Indian builds small fire—keeps warm sitting close. White man builds big fire—keeps warm chopping wood.'" And we laughed.

We had our little fire, made tea with water from a rivulet that threaded the meadow, and as darkness came on, we relished being in the high country, privileged by a sky dense with stars.

The next morning, Steve suggested we climb to the peak.

"It looks like a scramble up that talus slope," he said, pointing to the blue-shadowed slope, "and then work our way along the ridge to the top."

"I don't think I'll go," Bret said.

"Why not, brother?" I said. "Think of the view we'd have."

"I'd rather just be here," he said. This struck me as odd—why forego the best? Why break from the bond of brothers? But okay, have it your way.

Steve and I put snacks and water bottles into our packs and set off. The talus slope was shifty, but we made our precarious way up the steepening, balanced on moving scree, until we reached solid rock, and scrambled up to a hint of trail along the ridge. Now and then I paused to look down, find the speck of my brother first in camp, then out among the haze of flowers, lost in shadow under the trees.

Steve and I negotiated the knife ridge and made the final pitch to the peak. He was a longtime climber, assured. I was afraid, gripping every handhold tight, and only looking down at moments when I had a good purchase on the rock.

"Look here," Steve said at the pinnacle. From under a small pile of stones, he pulled an old peanut butter jar, with rusted lid and notes inside. "Climbers like to leave word," he said. "Nothing fancy, just proof and a name." We unfolded some of the notes carefully, so the wind wouldn't snatch them— pencil pale on candy wrappers, but heartfelt. Then we scrawled our own: "Steve and Kim were here. Beautiful day."

Somewhere, down low in the shadows, Bret was wandering among the trees. Not until later would I understand his reticence about the high place.

## "I NEVER WILL MARRY"

Knowing that my brother was about to move far north, I visited as often as I could. He lived with Lynne and Katie and Matt on Wedgwood Court in Salem, just east of the stately grounds of the State Mental Hospital, with its row of grand black walnut trees. The house itself was a low ranch with a small yard. There was a sliding glass door that faced south off the kitchen-dining room. My brother would sit by the glass with his guitar and sing the old Carter Family song:

> I never will marry, or be no man's wife.
> I expect to live single, all the days of my life. . . .

I didn't understand why he sang this song—as a man, as a married man. The tune was sweet and sad. The story was dark: the woman utters her vow, then throws herself into the waters to die.

Years before, when Bret was nine, he told our father, "I think I'll be a hermit when I grow up." As I listened to him sing, I remembered the day I had told my brother I was getting married, seventeen years before, in 1971.

"Beverly and I are getting married in Carmel, in August."

"You're getting married—before me?"

His first reaction had been about precedence, birth order, his assumed chronology of our lives.

"Well, yeah," I said. "It seems like the thing to do."

That day Bret sang in his winsome voice, looking out the window where sunlight spangled the leaves of the apple tree, I thought about the phrase "cut your expectations in half." I remembered that unfortunate line in my book of essays, *Having Everything Right*: "Part of our love must be to teach each other how to live alone."

While he sang, my wife, Beverly, and Bret's wife, Lynne, were doing dishes at the sink. Rosie was somewhere with Katie and Matt. I sat with my brother, foolishly admiring his facility with the guitar. The words did not manage to tell me what he would say to his brother. He sat straight, only his fingers moving, his gaze far away, his voice blending softly into the entrancing magic of his guitar.

Later that summer, before they packed and moved far north into Canada, Bret and Lynne came to Portland for a farewell breakfast with old family friends, Deborah and Becky Pauly, the sisters we thought we would marry when we were very young. They lived in France, in Paris and Bordeaux, but were home on a visit. We feasted at a place called L'Auberge, in northwest Portland. And after, we formed a circle in the parking lot, arms around shoulders, and uttered a series of vows: We would stay in touch. We would tell each other how it was. We would not break the circle of our childhood.

The next week my brother disappeared into the north country.

## SCUPPERS

When we were small, our parents read to us from the Little Golden Book called *Scuppers the Sailor Dog*. In those few pages, worlds opened, and our future was revealed: we would freely explore the world, saved by our wits and a frisky attitude. At a loss for direction? Let the wind decide. Shipwrecked? Be grateful to be alive. Marooned? Find an old chest half buried in the sand:

> Maybe it was treasure. It *was* treasure—to Scuppers. An old toolbox. . . .

So Scuppers built a house of drift wrack, and slept in comfort there. The image of him sprawled in delicious abandon on his bed of pine boughs in that catawampus hut always seemed the epitome of luxury to me. And then Scuppers took his tools, repaired his boat, and sailed serenely on.

Sorrow had a remedy and it was tools.

When my brother found a dog for his family, they named him Scuppers. Loyal friend.

Before departing for Canada, my brother went alone to the high country and camped for some weeks in the Goat Rocks Wilderness, in the Washington Cascades north of Mount Adams. He was simply gone into the spirit realm of that high, thin light. I was away somewhere and never learned the details of that adventure. But there is one dimension of the journey that I did hear.

When they went to meet my brother at the end of his trek, Lynne and Scuppers went up the trail from the parking lot near Trout Lake, and my brother—bearded, smoky from camp, and distilled to ethereal stuff by his time alone—came down the trail toward the south.

On that mountain trail they passed each other. Lynne did not recognize Bret. Bret did not recognize Lynne. And even Scuppers missed his master, so deeply disguised by mountain smoke was my brother then.

## "TO THINE OWN SELF"

As a teacher of the young, our mother had a metaphor she sometimes shared with parents: "We're trying to light candles, to help people feel warm and happy about themselves in their world—to become involved. We can light that candle in their heads and hearts." She sometimes added, when she discussed what a teacher offers, the concise proverb from E. M. Forster: "Only connect."

In one of his last letters home, my brother makes a crucial distinction between action and worth. When he had written our parents about his family's decision to move way north to Smithers, our mother had written back, with her thoughts, and her love, and Bret had immediately responded:

> Thanks so much for your supportive letter, which I just received. It
> meant a lot to me. . . . The main thing I appreciate about your letter
> is your support for ~~our decision, however it~~ us, and of course your
> affirmation of your love. I realize how important your approval/
> disapproval is to me. . . . There are many factors that went into the
> Smithers decision, as you probably appreciate. Mostly, I'm being true

to myself (as the good Shakespeare line says which you framed and gave to me when I was in high school).

The crossing out of "our decision," to be replaced by "us"—this feels like the most important clarity: "Your actions aside, I support you." When Polonius told his son Laertes, "To thine own self be true," he was offering a commonplace, but one that yet remains revolutionary. Our mother gave my brother the quotation, framed. He mentioned this in earlier letters. And he recalled it as he set off to go farther from us, it seems, than he could. And yet—and yet he was true to the self he knew, the Bret he knew, and we knew—the idealist, pacifist, historian, seeker after harmonious relations as the core value of his days.

## "GIVE ME YOUR NOTEBOOK"

That summer I went to a writing conference way out east in Wallowa County, Oregon—the Fishtrap Gathering. The bookstore was in a tepee, and the writing sessions were held in the big A-frame sanctuary at the old Methodist camp. It was a time for books in the making, big philosophy talk under the pines, stories and old-time music by the fire at night, and for me a predawn hike each morning alone up the rushing whitewater cataract pouring out of the mountains.

Through it all I was in pain. Life was killing me. Suffocation. Sleepless nights. For years I had held perverse pride in my marriage, no matter how hard it was. Divorce was for other people, lesser beings. I was loyal, I had staying power. When my wife told me adult life was like this—simply hard—I believed she must be right.

But on the last day of the conference, at a party high on the moraine, I overheard one of the writers, a stranger to me, holding forth fiercely about the imperatives of the intentional life. When she had a moment, I asked her out of the blue, "Would you have time to take a walk with me?"

We left the others, went out along the ridge, and helplessly I poured out my sorrow to her.

"I am faithful," I said. "I'm loyal to my wife and our child. I'm so lonely, but I don't sleep with anyone else. But sometimes I meet a friendly woman, and I start writing letters—not love letters, just friend letters. It's so good to have someone I can talk with, even far away."

"And your notebook," she said, "the one in your pocket over your heart— I see you take it out all the time and jot little things down."

"I can talk to my notebook," I said, "about anything."

We walked awhile in silence. Grasshoppers crackled up from the grass.

"I see you as this passionate person," she said, "who keeps his shirt buttoned to the top, like a preacher, restrained, impossibly good. And false."

We walked awhile. Then, abruptly, she turned to face me, extending her hand.

"Give me your notebook," she said.

"My notebook?"

"Give me your notebook," she said. "I won't read it, but I'm going to keep it for a month, then I'll mail it back to you. In these thirty days, don't write anything—no letters, no stories, no notebook. You have become a person who does not live. Instead, you write about living. You write a letter instead of having a relationship. You write a story about someone doing what you want to do. You write a poem out of longing, but you don't act. Words are not your friends right now. In this month, don't write about what you want to do. Do what you want to do. Every morning, when you wake up, think of what you want. Then either do that, or don't do that. Decide. But don't go sideways by writing about it."

My hand shook as I reached into my shirt pocket, but then I gave her the notebook, and she put it into her bag. We walked in silence back to the party, and she went her way.

As the gathering was breaking up, I stumbled down to the pond where others had been swimming earlier. In the hut, I put on my suit, left my clothes, and waded in. Was I strong enough to swim to the far side? I had to. The water was cold, dark. Halfway across, I thought I could not go on. My lungs burned, my arms were feeble ribbons. But somehow I struggled to the far shore, left the water, and stepped barefoot up the slope to the hilltop. As I had learned years ago from a Nez Perce friend, I turned to utter the blessing of the four directions, one by one:

> South, where summer bounty lies.
> West, the place of sunset and departure.
> North, where winter and privation teach us.
> East . . . from where the next thing comes, whatever that may be.

Below me on the slope, to the east, two fawns stepped out from the aspens, facing away from me. I was invisible to them. Their ears swiveled toward the last people at the party, across the lake. Their tails flickered, and one stamped a tiny hoof. Into my mind came the words: "my brother and me."

## RÉSUMÉ

My brother's life in Canada was good for a time, by the reports I heard. Lynne was teaching French Immersion, grades one and two, and their children, Katie and Matt, were in her school. Bret had time to fish the rivers, to read, and to hike in the woods. He had written our parents that our own early life in a small town had influenced the decision to move to Smithers: "I remember how large North Manchester and its snow and cozy feeling loomed in my childhood, and am hoping Katie and Matt will like Smithers." He noted that the small town in the empty north woods showed up on a world map "because there is a space to fill there." Maybe he would find work, he thought, as the town had a community college. After Bret headed north, I would get a postcard with a few words. Or by phone I would have a brief report.

But early that fall Bret appeared in Oregon. He wanted to come back, he told me. He needed to find work. It was not clear exactly what the plan was for the family, but he was serious about a job back home.

By the time he arrived, I had left my wife and child. My brother knew this, but not the whole story. The morning after I had surrendered my notebook at Fishtrap, with dawn came clarity: I needed to live alone. Back home, I had announced this to my wife, late at night, after Rosie was asleep.

"I have to do a trial separation," I said.

"Separation? What do you mean? Are you staying here tonight?"

"Okay, but in the morning I have to go."

"Maybe we should take that trip you talked about."

"We're past that."

"Will you give me the house?"

We lay down on the futon, inert. She held my hand in a grip, until she slept. In the morning, she took our daughter to school, and went to work. I gathered a few things into the car, and drove away.

I went that night to sleep in my office at the college, rolling out a sleeping bag on the floor. After a week, I found a little house to rent on southwest Custer Street, and moved a few things there. I had a bed, a table and a chair, and a couch. When my brother appeared from the north, he left his bag in my house, and we went to the college after work hours, to write his résumé. He had not seen my office there, so I showed him around.

"This is my desk, and over there is my assistant's desk. . . ."

His mouth was open. "This is your desk?" Then he was silent as I continued my list: my program newsletter, a list of courses we were offering, a grant I was writing.

I was blind. I was deaf. I was a fool as I babbled about the office. I did not see my brother, notice his quiet in the face of my speech. It wasn't until months later, I began to understand his silence as I conducted that tour: *So, little brother, you are teaching where our father taught. You have a job, a desk, an assistant, and a program. And I have nothing. I, your older brother, have nothing. I've thrown it all away.*

We sat down at my computer to make a résumé that might get him a planning job in Oregon again.

"So," I said, "for college—Grinnell was which year?"

"Don't list that," he said.

"Why not? You went there for your first year. It's a great school."

"Just don't list that," he said. "Do the U of O. . . ."

So we worked our way through his schooling—BA in sociology, University of Oregon . . . MA in anthropology, University of Victoria . . . MA in planning, Oregon State University. . . .

He told me he wanted two résumés—one for being a planner, and one for being a college teacher. "Probably community college."

"Let's make one draft with all the good stuff," I said, "and then customize for the two fields." So we did that. When he began to list what he did in his previous job, it sounded deadly to me:

> Responsible for preparing and presenting land use planning staff reports before elected and appointed officials. Writing administrative decisions. Coordinating planning activities with local and federal agencies. Administering the County Zoning Ordinance and explaining it to the public at the zoning counter. Responsible for guiding three other planners on staff regarding policy issues. 1981–1988.

I knew he was good at all those things, but his soul—my God, his soul had so much more to offer. I typed, and asked detail questions now and then, and typed some more. Then we made a draft letter of application for planning, and another for teaching. Our deal was that I would read the classified employment ads, and ask around about jobs, and call him with what I found. Then from Canada he would tell me what to send, and where.

When I thought we had what we needed, he told me to add a passage to the draft letter for planning: "I work well with elected and appointed officials, and have good public relations skills. I enjoy the planning process, and can work efficiently to meet deadlines and yet maintain the community relations essential to the long-range planning process."

Relations. Relationships. What about the life behind the work? I remember thinking these undeniable skills my brother held should be applied to life—not just the public business: "enjoy . . . efficient . . . relations . . . long-range." That was the trick, wasn't it—to be smart about the life, not just skilled in the work? And what about those "other interests" Bret listed at the bottom of his résumé: "Served as a big brother in the YMCA Big Brother program. Hiking, creative writing, guitar, and violin."

Big brother? That was his truth. So he was the best to me. But what about his relation to himself, his true self, the young animal ebullient in the wilderness I had known? Where was that creature in all this talk?

But what did I know? My own résumé, to be honest, would have to say: "Knows how to fool his way through a writing class, despite lack of real preparation, and cobble together a program on a wing and a prayer, clinging to a temporary job at the periphery of the college closest to where he grew up. . . ." As my friends had said, when they heard I was teaching where our father had taught, "The acorn never falls far from the tree."

When we had the draft pages done, we went back to my little bungalow, had a heap of spaghetti, and he settled on the couch for sleep, as I went to bed in my room. It had been a long day, and I was asleep the moment I hit the pillow.

Sometime after midnight, I heard my brother sobbing. The kind of sobbing that tries to be quiet, to not disturb, to hide. I went to him in the dark, held him in my arms where he curled, shaking on my lap. I could feel his ribs, he was so thin, and the shudder of his cries.

"I had a job," he sobbed, "a good job. I had a house, a retirement plan. I had an orthodontia plan, in case Katie and Matt—" He had to breathe, and sob. Then, when he got his breath, he went on. "I threw it all away, and now I have nothing. Lynne's happy. The kids are happy. I can't let them know I'm not happy. What can I do? What can—"

I held him, and held him, rocking him.

"It's all right," I said. "It will be all right. We'll get you a job. You can come back. You're so good—so good at what you do. You'll see, Bret. It will all be all right. . . ."

We were silent awhile, and he got his breath again.

"Bret, let's just go get your stuff," I said. "I'll drive you up to Smithers, we can get what you want, and come back to Oregon." He was silent. "That's what you want," I said. "Let's go together, and I'll bring you back, and then you can do job interviews. . . ."

"No," he said finally. "I don't need that. I'll go. I'll come back when there's an interview."

In the dark, feeling his ribs, sensing his despair, I realized I had a choice: I could take over my brother's life, maybe, and force him in the direction I knew was best. Or I could trust his way. I could either stop him from going alone, back to Canada, that remote town, that clink of the silverware, half expectation—or I could let him be my big brother, and go north alone.

I was too timid to do what I knew I should. Or I honored him, in ignorance, trusting what he said to reassure me, instead of living at the level of the heart with what I knew was needed.

I had held my brother. I had spoken comfort to him. I had assured him he could make his way into a new life. And I had lied, and by that lie betrayed him.

What I did not say that night was that by then I was not alone. Separated from my wife, then with another woman. Oh, I was very brave to set out on my own, camping out in my back-street rental and getting by on precious little—but by night I had help. I had pleasure. I had companionship that saved me, began to heal me from the wisp of man I had become. And yet of this I said no word to him. Instead, I urged him to be strong, to do what he needed to do.

In my darkest nights, when all my confidence falls away, I am convinced that by this lie, by this silence, by this dumb hypocrisy I killed my brother. I urged him to do the impossible, in ignorance, on trust.

After Bret headed north for Smithers, on my bookshelf I found a gift he had left me, a tiny birchbark canoe someone way up in Canada had made. Curled inside was a note in his dense script. There was a drawing of two figures in a canoe, with wavy lines for water carrying them along. Each raised a paddle. And the words:

Life's an adventure — what's around the next bend?
Thanks for the good time.

## BUS TAG

Bret loved the earth. To do this love right, by his estimation, meant an exacting vigilance against the self. Up north in Smithers, I am told, he would not light a fire in the fireplace, as this would pollute the atmosphere. He lived in a forest. Wood everywhere. Cold. But no fire.

When he took a journey by bus, he filled out his address on the tiny paper luggage tag with the elastic string. When he moved, and took the bus again, he did not get a new tag. He crossed out his old numbers and wrote new ones on the old tag. I have it still. It is a testament.

## "YOU CAN'T BUY THIS SONG"

So my brother went back to Smithers, and I set out on a journey—flying to Boston for the annual meeting of the American Folklore Society, and from there to San Diego where I would be trained to offer public programs about American writers. We were put up at the Coronado Del Rey, the classic old hotel with a set of free in-room movies that had all been filmed at the hotel. In the morning, dolphins flashed through the waves just offshore, the food was opulent, appointments lavish. I learned by the luck of the draw I was to master the work of Sylvia Plath and deliver a program at Central Library in Portland a month later.

At the meeting, I fell into conversation with a brilliant writer named Diane Middlebrook, on the faculty at Stanford, who had published a book about Anne Sexton. On the beach, barefoot, watching the dolphins play, we spoke of suicide—a mysterious topic that Sexton and Plath had brought into any discussion of modern American poetry. She had theories; I had ignorance. The topic seemed so far away, but I was grateful to have some ideas to weave into my lecture on Plath's *Ariel* in Portland very soon.

It was Halloween, and four of us—Diane and I and two others—decided to go to Tijuana for the night. Someone had a rented car, and we headed south, left the car at the border, crossed into Mexico on foot, split up at a certain street corner, and agreed to meet there again at 2 a.m. to head back north.

This was my cup of tea. I could not be a good teacher, I could never be the writer our father was, I couldn't solve my brother's life. But I did know how to wander.

First off, I needed to go into the cathedral to watch the wedding that music announced was happening. I sat in the back, beside a man eating a whole chicken. There seemed to be a big family for the marriage, and also a lot of strangers, like me, moths drawn to the flame. The organ played, the priest spoke at length, the bride was beautiful and the groom handsome.

From there I went to a jai alai match at a club down the street, watching in complete ignorance as two young athletes hurled the *pelota* with their long wands of reed. I sat behind a screen with a few others, our heads swiveling in unison as the ball streaked, pocked savagely against the wall, and ricocheted in a new trajectory.

When I came out from the court, it was evening, and many on the street wore masks, and sold masks, especially to gringos like me. Should I be wolf, saint, king? I declined, and walked on. My goal was to get almost lost—right out there at the periphery. The boundary was the center for me then. And when I reached the far edge of comfort, I was home.

Tacked to a telephone pole, I saw a song, "A Mi Tijuana Querida" (To My Beloved Tijuana). The song praised the town as a woman—smiles like the sun, glances of love, a mother's bounty. At the bottom of the sheet was written:

*Letra y música de Rafa de Tijuana.*
*Tijuanense ésta es tu canción — cántala*
*como quieres! como un corrido.*
*Esta canción no puedes comprar — es por tí.*

"You can't buy this song. It is for you."

By the time I rejoined my friends for the sleepy ride north, I was at the center of myself, filled with music, confident in beauty, possessed with an ability to love.

My friend back in Portland was waiting for my return. She was so kind to me. This is the life I would lead: new love, songs, wandering, teaching. And out of this confidence in myself, surely I could guide my brother back to safety. Life was so filled with beautiful experience, the good temptations of pleasure and creation could do miracles with him, as they had with me.

But why, why did I not tell my brother all this? I lied with silence.

## "DO YOU EVER HUNT WITH A PISTOL?"

I returned to Portland, dithered in my own world, didn't call the family. Give myself some space, I thought. I spent the night with my love, woke with a sense of bounty, new life. It was November 7, 1988. I walked from her house to mine, and there, as I opened the door, the phone was ringing. It was Mother.

"You'd better come here. Something terrible has happened."

My mind went through the list—our father, gone? My beloved Aunt Helen, gone? Family friends . . . the dog? Not for a moment did I think of my brother, and then she said, "It's Bret . . . killed himself . . . at Kit's."

Our father was away—in Iowa—but would catch the next flight. My sisters were at home, with mother. I drove there, we cried, huddled, stunned.

Gradually, they pieced together what had happened while I was away—in California, and with my secret love. Bret had come home to Oregon. Thanks to the letters I had sent for him, he had two job interviews, one in Hood River, where he had worked in the past, and one in Redmond, in central Oregon, a few miles from where our sister Kit was living with her boyfriend, Dan.

Sister Barb's husband, Steve, agreed to drive Bret to the interviews. The journey was often silent, Steve had reported. He couldn't get Bret to talk. At the first interview, in Hood River, we learned later that people on the committee knew Bret, and liked him, believed he could do the job. But he was catatonic. Barely mumbled answers to questions. They wanted to hire him, but they could not.

Steve and Bret headed up over Mount Hood, down through the Warm Springs Indian Reservation, and south through Madras. Again, Steve tried to get Bret to talk, but there was not much there. Depression was that deep, and we did not know its name.

The only time on the journey Bret got active was south from Madres, as they approached the bridge over the Crooked River—a place we had stopped as kids to let our gaze fall far down to the dim blue thread of water deep in that gorge. Bret wanted to stop. It was the first time on their journey he had come to life about something. Steve said they walked to the middle of the bridge, and Bret looked down. No words. Just a long gaze. They stood there, stood there.

Then they went on to Redmond. Bret was dressed up, looked ready. But again, in the interview he was severely reserved. His qualifications looked good, but people on the committee told me later there was no way they could offer him a job. He just wasn't alive to their questions.

From there, Steve drove Bret to Kit's place. She was away, and Dan was away. What should Bret do?

Steve offered to drive him back to Portland, or leave him there for a visit with Kit. Bret couldn't decide. They got his suitcase out of the car. It seemed he was going to carry it to the house, but instead he stood in the yard, holding the suitcase. I see him in that yard in the tableau of his confusion, a diorama that will burn in my mind forever.

"What shall I do?" he said.

"Whatever you want to do," Steve said. "I'm ready either way." I imagine he faced the same dilemma I had: take over, or let Bret decide.

In the end, Bret decided to stay, Steve drove west for home in Portland. After a time, Dan came home, welcomed Bret, made lunch, opened a couple beers. But like the others, he couldn't get much from Bret. Just a few syllables. So, like a good host, Dan kept the conversation moving—reporting on his veterinary work, his horses, what he and Kit had been doing. Among many things, he reported they had been duck hunting. This was the only time in the conversation Bret seemed to rise from his paralysis.

"Do you ever hunt with a pistol?" he said.

"Well . . . I have a pistol," Dan said, "but I wouldn't use it to hunt ducks."

From there, Bret sank back into silence, and eventually Dan had to get back to work. He assured Bret that Kit would be home soon, and was eager to see her brother. She was shopping for a good meal that night, and they would have a fine time.

Sometime after Dan left the house, and before Kit returned, my brother made a systematic search. He knew there was a pistol somewhere. Finally, there it was, in a boot, under the bed.

When Kit came in, he was dead—blood, pistol, silence.

## WOMAN RCMP

Our father would be home soon, but it was clear to me I had to call my brother's wife. How to do this? First I called and called until I got the Royal Canadian Mounties.

"My brother has taken his life," I said. "I have to call his wife in Smithers. I want a woman officer outside the house before I call—to help, if there is need. Can you do this?"

The answer was yes, and in twenty minutes I had a call back that the officer was there.

When Lynne answered the phone, I told her I had some hard news. "Bret took his life—at Kit's. I'm so sorry . . ."

"He tried that up here," she said, "but it didn't work."

"What? Tried what?"

"He took the car and a paper bag out a forest road, and tried breathing the fumes to die. But he passed out and just fell over. Then he drove home."

"Why didn't you tell me that?"

"I was teaching, or I was home. I didn't want him to hear me calling you, and at work. . . ."

"But Lynne, you had to call."

"Like I said, I couldn't." Her voice was level, as if she knew the news before I called.

"At night," she said, "after the kids were asleep, he would walk back and forth at the foot of the bed in his underwear, wringing his hands, repeating over and over, 'What shall I do? What shall I do?'"

"Why didn't you call me?"

"Like I said . . ."

"Well, Lynne," I said, "can you and the kids come down?"

"Yes, of course."

"How soon?"

"I'll have to see."

I told her there was an RCMP car outside, in case she needed to talk with someone. She said she would be all right, and we said goodbye.

## THE GOOD TIME

At the memorial service, our father, the great poet, the man of words, whose many poems counsel connection, bravery, and affection even in strange and difficult times—this great man could not sit with us. He was somewhere at the back of the chapel, roving the boundary. I glimpsed him now and then as we said our words about my brother, as friends from all over spoke their stories and their love—and then I looked back and our father was gone.

Since then, it has come to me that his own unspoken tragedy may have been his failure to save his own brother—Bob, in Kansas, father of nine, who drank himself to death in 1965, twenty-three years earlier. I've since learned that after Bob's death, when our father went to Kansas for the service, my nine cousins confronted him.

"You were supposed to take care of him," they said. "You were older. You were successful. He had his troubles. Why didn't you take care of your brother?"

After Bret's death, our father went into seclusion, spending time in his study with the door closed. It was never closed before—always open to us, no matter how busy he might be. But this time, he was in there reading Wordsworth, clawing for some way forward. And when he emerged at last, he would not speak of Bret. Changed the subject when mourners came. Kept a brittle jolly banter going, as time moved on.

We learned later he could talk with people far away, on his frequent travels for poetry and teaching. It wasn't until after he died, five years later, in 1993, that I began to receive reports of these conversations. And then the poem:

A MEMORIAL: SON BRET

In the way you went you were important.
I do not know what you found.
In the pattern of my life you stand
where you stood always, in the center,
a hero, a puzzle, a man.
What you might have told me
I will never know — the lips went still,
the body cold. I am afraid
in the circling stars, in the dark,
and even at noon in the light.
When I run what am I running from?
You turned once to tell me something,
but then you glimpsed a shadow on my face
and maybe thought, Why tell what hurts?
You carried it, my boy, so brave, so far.

Now we have all the days, and the sun
goes by the same; there is a faint
wandering trail I find sometimes, off
through grass and sage. I stop
and listen: only summer again — remember? —
The bees, the wind.

Our father reached back to good times. He reached toward his silent son. He accused himself. He addressed the boy, age forty, tenderly, in a way he could not speak to us. "You turned once to tell me something." How many times, telescoping back through years, do I now see that hesitation in my brother's face? Some things never said.

After the service, after Lynne and Katie and Matt had returned to Smithers, and the Stafford family struggled to find simple days somehow, I was in my house, rattling around, sorting ordinary things.

On the bookshelf was the little birchbark canoe Bret had left me. Wanting to touch what he had touched, I picked it up. I had forgotten the note there, curled like a shaving of wood. I unrolled the little scroll, saw again his drawing of the canoe with two paddlers—my brother and me—and read the words again:

Life's an adventure — what's around the next bend?
Thanks for the good time.

But now, my eye tapered for the finest touch of his spirit, I saw the winsome little loop at the end of that last word, and recognized his farewell to his little brother:

Thanks for the good times.

Saying goodbye to me for good, my brother was sending me back, far back into our lives when we were pals, back to all the good times then.

# BOOK II. GOD BLESS YOU

# POEMS FOR GRUBIA

Years after my brother had died, and after our father had died, a little book turned up that our father had made before Bret was born. Typed and stapled together, it was a one-of-a-kind collection of our father's earliest poems— poems written while he was interned as a conscientious objector, a C.O., during World War II. On the cover of the book, he had typed, "Words One Summer / By Bill E. Stafford." And inside, a dedication page:

for Grubia . . . and
Dorothy & Meager

When I asked our mother about this, she explained. "We were standing on a bridge, just after the war. Maybe it was Elgin—in Illinois. We got to talking about having children. We'd each had three in our families—my brother and sister, his brother and sister—and we decided it would be best if we had four—one more. But what about names? Somehow, we came up with the name Grubia. It was kind of a joke—Grubia. Just like our other idea: 'Meager.' We thought we might have twins—two boys: Eager and Meager. Or maybe Flawless and Lawless." She laughed her musical laugh. "So the book was for the children yet to be."

That scene in Elgin, though, was later. For this little book is dated 1944, the war still on, and many things uncertain. He was still interned in camp, earning an allowance of $2.50 per month. Prospects were slender, but imagination alive. Our father-to-be wrote in his preface to the book:

There are innumerable worlds around us all the time, just waiting to be discovered by the right squint of the beholder; and when I don't say my words right, some of those worlds might as well not even be created, for they will never be known. Some worlds are hard to see, and some are so easy that we have seen them too often. Everyone, of course, finds many of those worlds. I want to share mine.

And farther along in the book, bound in the war, our father is afraid to hope for us:

> My farm on tealwing river
> is a picture farm,
> Spread on comely hills
> like rich brocade . . .
>
> There is a woman there
> through a window of light
> And a child like a promise. All
> without a sound.
>
> There is my farm in that valley,
> but I dare not go there.
> It always is there in the distance,
> and I dare not go near.

I remembered the story of our parents' first meeting, a year earlier, in 1943. He was in the C.O. camp in the hills above Santa Barbara, and she the pretty minister's daughter when he came to preach to the boys. Our father spotted her, and asked, "Would you like to take a walk?" They went up along a dusty road. The moon was on the rise. At some distance, they saw dust rising along a road, and one began to quote a sentence from a Willa Cather story, "Two Friends," from the book *Obscure Destinies*. One started the sentence, and the other completed it verbatim—and their recognition of each other was sealed. Later, they sat on the lawn in camp. The window of the music building was open, and someone had the Grieg Piano Concerto in A on the phonograph. And that was that. They exchanged letters, telegrams, visits—and very soon they were married.

After years of savoring this story, I thought to track down the passage in "Two Friends." The beginning is romantic and resonant with affection. But as the passage continues, things go deeper:

> More than once, in Southern countries where there is a smell of dust and dryness in the air and the nights are intense, I have come upon a stretch of dusty white road drinking up the moonlight beside a blind wall, and have felt a sudden sadness. Perhaps it was not until the next morning that I knew why,   and then only because I had dreamed of Mr. Dillon or Mr. Trueman [the two friends] in my sleep. When that old scar is occasionally touched by chance, it rouses the old uneasiness; the feeling of something broken that could so easily have been mended, of something delightful that was senselessly wasted, of a truth that was accidentally distorted—one of the truths we want to keep.

The story ends there, and Cather appends the line "Pasadena 1931." Pasadena, near where our mother was living at the time.

And like that passage, the early love of our parents was not simple. There was poverty, postwar dim prospects for a pacifist, and then a miscarriage. There was negotiation between them about how to live, and for our father, what he was allowed to write about, and for our mother, how she was to behave with this poet, this artist. They separated for a time. It was the warmth of California and home for our mother, and the privations of Midwest winter in Illinois for our father. But in time the dusty white road brought them back together, and the family began.

After my brother died, I asked our father why I had survived.

"Bret was a saint," he said. "You're not. That's good."

Was Grubia the miscarried soul? Eager and Meager—were they my brother and me? We both started eager. Flawless and Lawless? I know who was who in that equation.

## OUR SKY

Bret's beginning was in Oregon, where the folks lived in a little rental in the sleepy town of Lake Grove, a few miles from the college where our father taught. Another family nearby, the Paulys, were close friends—Reinhard taught at the college, too, in the Music Department, and Connie bore their first child, Deborah, a few days after Bret was born. The Stafford house was a casual affair. It is reported you could lay a spool on the living room floor and it would roll to the low spot. But what matter? The men had jobs, the women had babies, and it was summertime, 1948.

My own beginning was in Oregon, where we lived at another old house, on southwest Palatine Hill Road, just south of the cemetery, and closer to the college. And shortly after I was born, the Paulys had their second child, Rebecca. The world was taking shape in balance for our destiny.

They tell me there was a great cherry tree in the yard outside my room. When they would lay me on my back in my crib, I would look up into the spangled light of that tree, staring and staring as the gold sun flickered through the blossoms in spring, and the leaves in summer. That was my sky.

There seemed to be a tug-of-war all through our childhoods—the Midwest of our parents' heritage tugging us to the open land, and the West Coast of their meeting and marriage tugging them back to the West. Whatever the reason, we got good at the rhythm of goodbye, then starting over in a new house, a new place to explore. Our father said he learned the hard way that one must arrive in the new town in the morning—after a good night's sleep, and a good breakfast. Otherwise, "the year to follow will never be successful."

How did this pattern of migration shape our little lives? We had to leave Deborah and Becky behind, and find new friends. We had to start over, but we had the family, always the family—like a trusty spaceship roaming the galaxy.

I search those early years for clues, for the trick of beginning in my brother's character, and in mine. My brother loved dogs. For a few days when we were young, we kept a big Samoyed we named Shadow who appeared in our yard. My brother signed a note from that sweet interim, "From Bret, and Shadow." Then the owners appeared, and Shadow went home.

Bret loved cars. An early game was to sit in a toy car and make the sound of the almost-defeated starter motor: "*Rur, rur, rur, ruuuur.* Uh, oh. Out of gas." He made little books telling the history of different models, and an elaborate hand-drawn guide to the distinguishing fins, fenders, and head- and taillights of a Dodge, a Plymouth, a Ford, and a Cadillac. In another book, he reports that "The first Ford went 25 feet (*put . . . put*—crash)." In yet another little book he detailed the history of the car as a process of adding parts: The first car, he reported, had three wheels. Then "At last a man made a car that had four wheels. . . . A man made a car with a pump [the Stanley Steamer]. . . . A man made a car with a windshield . . . a roof . . . a spare tire. . . ." He liked how history could give you a sense that things could proceed by relatively simple means, and to arrive at a complex goal. Cars could take you far, and maybe growing up could be like this process of addition.

He seemed to fancy journeys. He loved maps, bought himself a little implement you could adjust for scale and roll across a map to learn the exact distance from one place to another. There is something in the family's yo-yo rhythm of migration that prefigures my brother's later pattern of traveling in search of independence and then returning home in search of security.

In one of our early migrations, when we left Iowa for Oregon again, little Bret wistfully asked, as he surveyed the new place, "Does our sky hook onto Donna's sky?" Donna had been his friend in Iowa. This question strikes me as foundational: Does my experience have continuity? Are my friends and consolations in a far place, a far time, still within reach for me? Am I the same person—does my own sky hook together? Can I have what I want? Can I always love what I once held close?

## LOST WORDS

Our father was a traveler, a seeker. As my brother said in a letter sent the spring before he died, after a visit to Lake Oswego, "We're sorry you weren't home to enjoy our cup of cocoa too, Daddy. But we trust you were having a rewarding expedition as you always do."

Before our father was famous and a frequent traveler, with the National Book Award for poetry in 1963, he had time to listen to us very closely, and his journal of our utterance, together with our mother's record, both give me a glimpse into that formative time. We pondered our father's pacifism in a world prone to anger and strident ways. One night, our parents overheard us arguing in the dark after we had gone to bed:

> *Kim:* I don't want to kill anybody, even if someone tries to take over our country.
>
> *Bret:* God is on the side of the good country; he guides Theodore Roosevelt and Abraham Lincoln and George Washington. . . .
>
> *Kim:* He guides the people who don't want to kill, too.
>
> *Bret:* But they aren't famous.

The notion of the obscure work of peace was a thread that started early. To deny oneself the luxury of anger—that was a trick we had to learn.

When Bret was three, he announced, "You don't stand in a dark wind." He wanted the world to be an inclusive place: "Let's make a hole in our house so a rat can come in and live."

One time, Bret was told not to eat the pears under a tree by our house. Then he was observed picking one up. But then he noticed the observer— and flinging the pear from his hand, he said sternly, "Way, pears!" Go away, temptation. Go away, what I want. His was a sterner code than mine.

> *Bret:* Kim, why don't you be nice—like God?

I had to find my consolations, to possess wild food for my soul:

> Kim: This has been an awful good day. First I found a snake,
> then an old rotten dried up mouse, then a baby dead
> mole and then an old part of a gun. The snake will
> probably get away. A cat will eat the dried up mouse.
> The baby dead mole's mother will take him to her nest.
> But I'll keep the old part of a gun!
>
> Kim: *(when he got mad)* I'll go outdoors and just keep on
> walking.

My brother, on the other hand, held out for a world where beauty and honor would prevail, as when he asked, "Does something ever look so pretty robbers won't tear it down?" All his life, my brother lived this question. Could something in the world be so right, so worthy, so deserving it would survive: land-use plans, wild places, native values, one's own belief in self, in life? Could something in himself be so pure, so tender, so gentle—and yet find a place in the long siege of adult life: peace, old home, beauty? He began his quest early and was persistent.

It was against our code to dislike anyone. It was all love among the Staffords. But for me, love had strategic gradations:

> Kim: *(telling about Gary hitting him in the nose at school)*
> You know, there are some people I just like instead of
> love—like Gary.

What could be the future for two boys close in age, small but united in the big world?

> Bret: Will you marry me, Kim?
> Kim: I can't marry you because I'm not a mother.
> Bret: Sure you can, 'cause you have curly hair like a mother.
> Kim: But I wouldn't have any babies inside me.

*Bret:* Oh well, we could steal one from the doctor.

When our sisters, Kit and then Barbara, arrived, they had rich thoughts in the mix as well:

> *Kit:* Daddy, why is God such a good boy?
>
> *Barbara:* These are *wild* flowers? Do they bite?

We were four by then, and we turned outward to address the world. When it was just my brother and me, we were like two pillars forming a tent of knowing, and we relied on each other.

> The boys play a fine game they invented for bedtime. With the lights off, they lie in bed and play their records. Bret: *Push in the needle, turn on the record player, here goes.* Kim sings the only song he knows: *My country, 'tis of thee . . . to sleep, sleep on mother's breast,* loud and off-key. When he finishes, he says in a low voice, *Bottom, bottom, bottom, bottom,* while Bret says, *That's all, turn off the record player, click. Now for. . . .* (off to sleep).

My project was to understand how all this fits together. Dreams seeped into days, and days were bowls to hold mystery. One time, coming out from my nap, I rubbed my eyes and told our father, "Bill, you know what? God is dead."

> *Kim:* What if when we think we are awake we are dreaming,
>         and when we're dreaming we are awake?

In two little books my brother and I made in 1953, my brother has drawn a self-portrait, identified in our mother's note as "Me taking a walk to school." The figure has a flat line for a mouth, and hands held high—in warning, greeting, or defense? The family story is that Bret took one look at the bus driver that year, did not trust his face, and decided he would walk to school instead.

My own book is filled with dreamy lines and dots, which our father's transcript reports to be "river . . . moon . . . boat . . . someone walking in the rain . . . stars & footprints."

Trying now, at sixty-two to sort out my brother's life of mysterious magic, and his trick of death, I'm still groping for firsthand information about the invisible.

> *Kim:* (*age seven*) Mama, is Grandpa in Heaven?
>
> *Dorothy:* Many people think that is what happens when you die.
>
> *Kim:* But, Mama, what do you think?
>
> *Dorothy:* I don't really know, Kim, but a good part of growing up is that people get to decide what they believe about all those big questions.
>
> *Kim:* Well, the next person who dies, I'm going to hang on his feet and find out.

In one of his own last letters home, my brother closes with an account of reading from his own record to his children:

> This evening, Katie and Matt asked me to read in my journal about what they said when they were really little kids (Voices Remembered—Generation Two). They laughed away as I read such things as Matthew's version of verse two of "Jingle Bells." His goes ". . . making syrups bright."

There is the link that yet amazes me: the parent hears the child's inventive code, writes it down, and passes it along.

> *Bret:* You have nice boys of us.

## CHEATING DEATH

When my brother was maybe two years old, he performed a parent's worst nightmare—running out with exuberant glee between two parked cars into a busy street. As our father described the incident later, "A saint was driving by, jammed on his brakes, and Bret was saved. Only a saint would be alert enough to see that little tyke."

Shortly after this close call, we moved into the house in Tualatin, then a sleepy crossroads that consisted of a tavern, a bridge over the river, and a railroad crossing. While everyone else was busy unpacking the car, I went to explore the backyard. Eventually, the folks came calling, seeking me. As our mother told the story later, they found me sitting on a cracked board over an abandoned well, dropping pebbles one by one into the dark shaft, and listening for the plop of water far below.

After such beginnings, every day, every summer, every act was a bonus in the world where we had the long-odds good luck to live. Our mother had very nearly died at birth in a farmhouse in rural Nebraska. Our father had almost been hung by a mob in Arkansas for being a pacifist in the wrong place at the wrong time during the war. My brother came close to death in several fire-fighting encounters when he worked for the Forest Service. And later, I fell asleep at the wheel of my VW bug at 3 a.m., driving north from L.A. when I was in college. I came awake to see bushes in a blur flying by on both sides.

At two, you run between parked cars. You survive, and live on for a time, a golden time, your run of precious luck.

## "COME ON IN"

When my brother and I were small, our mother made a book of photographs positioned on folds of blue construction paper by red brackets at each of the four corners. On the cover is the classic photo of my brother, age two. He has crawled into the kitchen cupboard, leaving a scattering of pans on the floor. His face shows settled confidence. He has made a world by removing what doesn't fit. In his stripy shirt, short pants, and sandals, he looks back over his shoulder at us all. Under the photo, our mother has written, "Come On In."

The two of us sit side by side on the couch, with our handmade Halloween masks. I am a pig and he is a cat—or a fox, or a wolf, or a dog. It's hard to tell. And then we are in the pile of leaves outside, my brother grinning, and I with a pensive mouth.

Then we stand before our parents in our dark jumpsuits, stuffed into hats and mittens. Behind our family quartet, icicles four feet long descend from the eave of the Quonset hut in our Midwest winter. Daddy is getting his PhD, while Mother teaches school. There in the next image stands her wintry school, and then the living room strewn with toys.

But the classic image, to me, is the one where my brother and I sit naked in the double sink against the Quonset's inward-sloping wall. I'm the pudgy one with curly hair, Bret the one with the big smile. Something about the image, and the moment, catches me every time: we fit side by side, and will always.

The book closes with the opening image a second time: my brother reigning supreme from inside his cupboard kingdom. Below this photo, this our mother has written in her flowing script:

> We like to invite you in
> and you see it's cozy
> where people are friendly
> just the way
> it's always been.

Such a book preserves what was: love, hope, icicles, and our little house of tin.

## THE INDIAN BLANKET

That night it was tall and full of lights, the hospital freckled with windows.

"Stay here," our father said. "See that window five floors up, out at the end? That's where Dorothy is. Do you have the Indian blanket wrapped around you snug? Good boys." The door closed slowly, clicked.

He went off through the dark parking lot. My brother and I were in the backseat of the old Dodge, the car Grandpa gave us, the one where I spilled applesauce on the upholstery, where my baby bottle froze crossing Iowa because the heater didn't work. Our father was going up to our mother. Was my brother afraid? Was I? I can't remember. Our sister Kit had just been born. Why didn't our father take us up there to see? The world was a safe place then. You could leave your children in the car in the parking lot at night, out behind Good Samaritan. Who would harm them?

We held the hem of the Indian blanket to our chins. My brother was a warm animal beside me. I was not the youngest anymore. There was a baby, and she was up there in the lights.

## THE SMARTEST PET

At school there was a contest, and my brother took his pet snake, Towey, in a shoebox. In the course of the day, with birds and cats and dogs and fish in bowls all jostling for admiration, Towey escaped inside the classroom. There was a big search with everything turned topsy-turvy, but Towey was not found.

When it came time for the awards ceremony, Bret was crestfallen. His teacher, alert to what was at stake, invented a new category: the Smartest Pet. Towey, clever enough to escape, took the prize. If you can't be good, at least you can get away.

Later, Bret had a white rat he loved. The creature would nuzzle around Bret's neck. Then there was the turtle named Binoculars. Eventually, our father brought home an Airedale puppy he named Beau and we called Bo.

My brother made a book of yellow paper stapled together, about the size of a seven-year-old's palm, with drawings of dog and master. The text of this manual has the beautiful blend of authority and compassion that was our childhood:

If you have a dog that you would like to train I will show you how.
First you must put your dog's leash on like this.
Then you must get something that your dog likes to eat.
Then say heel. Heel means for the dog to stay by you.
If the dog does heel give it something.
Keep on doing that for about a half hour for 3 days.
Next tell your dog to sit for 2 days.
Then tell your dog to stay in one place and you go to another.
Then tell your dog to come.
You can teach your dog to jump or anything you want to but
    be gentle.

Years later, a family dog named Nicholas Baranoff, or Nick, ran off and disappeared in the countryside south of where we lived in Oregon. Bret was in college by then and decided to find that dog. On his bike, he went from farm to farm, working his way systematically across the landscape in a widening circle. Eventually, he met a farmer who had sheep. My brother described Nick, our regal Siberian husky, definitely an alpha male.

"Son," the farmer said, "a great big dog that looked a lot like that was running my sheep, and I shot him. He's buried up on the hill. If that's your dog, you owe me the price of some sheep. Shall we continue this conversation?"

My brother turned from the farm and rode home.

## THE LIE

There is no question I could be "a bad boy." Such a useful phrase, the identification for a role in the stage play of daily life: Bad Boy.

In my career, I have participated in shoplifting, lying, deflecting blame to the innocent, and "pretending" to light my sister on fire after my friend Van and I had tied her to the tetherball pole in fierce play. I got raked over the coals for that one, and was forbidden to carry matches—which, to that point, had been one of several essentials I always carried as a good Boy Scout, trying to be prepared at all times to do good.

Our parents had definite ideas about raising us, many of them lifted, though modified, from the books of Dr. Spock and Rudolf Dreikers. Dreikers, in particular, in a series of books including *Children: The Challenge*, *The Challenge of Marriage*, *The Challenge of Parenthood*, and others, offered scenarios of good and bad parenting for consideration, along with a set of principles for moving from parenting by hierarchical authority to parenting by democratic means with logical consequences. When I peruse his books now, struggling to be a decent parent for my son, Guthrie, I come upon much familiar terrain: "Avoid Power Struggles," "Win Cooperation," "Don't Shoo Flies," and "Maintain Routine." All these are familiar. The one primary dimension of Dreikers' approach that I don't remember is the "Family Council," a weekly opportunity for each child and each parent to take turns raising issues and proposing solutions—solutions that the family is required, on principles of democratic fairness, to try out together. I remember plenty of counsel, but I don't remember a regular habit of councils.

How did all this work, in practice? When I was good, all flowed serenely. And other times . . . well, it got complicated.

For my fifth birthday, in the little town of North Manchester, Indiana, I got a gun. We had ridden our bikes out to a favorite place, a railroad bridge over a lazy stream I remember being called the Kenapocomoco River. On the riverbank, near the railroad bridge just outside town, we had a picnic under the bare cottonwood trees. Then our father produced from some hidden place a long package. I tore it open, and there was my prize. He showed me how to pump it up, aim it away from everyone, and pull the trigger. A burst of air made a satisfying *Bang!*

"Even though it doesn't shoot anything," he said, "never aim at anyone. That's basic about a gun, any gun." I nodded. That made sense to me, for the moment.

Now when we played Davy Crockett, or Daniel Boone, I had the real thing. We could swagger down the alley toward the Cumberland Gap, or cross the school field to find the Alamo, and I carried the lightning stick that made stubby little me something to reckon with. Sometimes I let Bret use it, but most of the time he just had to use a stick and pretend it was a real gun like mine.

I don't remember how I developed my special trick with the gun, playing alone. Maybe I stumbled once and dropped it muzzle-first into the dirt, wedging a plug of earth at the end of the barrel. But the next time I pulled the trigger, that plug of earth went flying. Now *that* was fine.

I kept this technique to myself, not even showing my brother. I got scientific about it, testing different kinds of earth, trajectories of aim, number of pumps at the air chamber. Then came the showdown.

The family was in a park in town, scattered, exploring. I saw a car coming. Indians! I plugged my rifle with earth, pumped five, then six times, and crouched behind a tree in my best Daniel Boone fashion. As the band of Indians in the round gray Dodge passed, I fired. Bull's-eye!

There was a screech of brakes, and a man in a long wool coat jumped out, sucking furiously on his pipe as he strode in my direction. I ran for our father.

"Your boy shot my car," the man said. I could hear his teeth clicking on the pipestem. I looked at the ground.

Our father the pacifist adopted his best level voice to de-escalate the situation. Taking the gun from me, he explained that it was just an air rifle. Carefully pointing it away from anyone, he pumped it twice, and pulled the trigger. The gun gave a genteel pop.

"That's all it does," our father said.

"Well, something hit my car."

"Did you aim the gun at this man's car?" our father said to me.

Head down, I nodded. "I'm sorry if I aimed at your car, Mister," I said.

The man looked at me, at the gun in our father's hands, and then into our father's eyes. "I don't think your boy's ready for a gun," he said. "Of course that's your affair. Just my opinion." A couple puffs on the pipe, and then he strode back to his car and drove away.

Our father knelt down beside me and handed me the gun, but when I took it he was still holding his end. "How did he get the idea that you shot something at him?" he said.

I shook my head and shrugged.

## ROPE IN THE RIVER

On one of the many cross-country journeys between the Midwest and the West Coast, we stopped in Jackson Hole, Wyoming, to camp. While the folks raised the tent, Bret and I set out to explore. At a foamy, white stream we decided we had to see what was on the far side. Fortunately I had a rope, and we tied an end around Bret's waist and an end around mine.

Being oldest, he went first, wading into the cold rush to his knees, and then to his waist. He stumbled then, and I braced myself as he disappeared under the water. I saw the rope throb, anchored to my greatest treasure in the roiling deep.

I played him like a fish, skidding down loose dirt, scrabbling for my footing. That day, the current swept him in an arc toward the bank, and I pulled him free.

## TREASURE THIEF

I have realized only recently that in my childhood we were poor. Maybe we felt rich because we lived with bountiful stories, ideas, places. Abundance was everywhere—the sky, rivers with their infinitely changing ways, mornings in summer that lasted longer than a life. Our kin in Kansas were myriad—nine cousins in one big house! And there was a generous air about our lives that everything was possible, as long as you paid attention to what was right. Limited means in some cases resulted in unlimited power. From that time, I remember a toy that put all we could not have in the shade. When you held it in your hand, you could not believe it: a tiny Studebaker that was a working harmonica—pipes along the rear bumper, and when you blew a tune, the headlights shone. Which millionaire's car could do that?

But there just wasn't much money. After our father died, I found his accounting for a series of his transactions on the back of a poem from those early days. After a tall column of figures, he owed the secretary of the English Department three cents for a stamp.

Maybe this—our spare means but expansive spiritual entitlement—led to my crime wave in grade two. Shoplifting, lying about found money, the stolen Bible from church—these episodes in my biography contrasted with my brother's ways. As the young saint, he watched me falter, counseled me to do right, threatened to tell on me, but did not follow through.

That year, 1957, in San Jose my brother kept a diary faithfully for an astounding forty-eight-day run. The diary has month and day marked out neatly on half pages: March 17 . . . March 18 . . . March 19, and so on. The dates are filled in with pen all the way into June, while the daily reports are in either pen or pencil. Apparently, he marked out the days all in one go, and then wrote a sentence, or at least a few words, for every day from March 17 until May 4.

From this record I am reminded of our cave in the backyard. And that we "built a house" every second or third day—several times reported to be two stories high, but once revealed to top out at an altitude of four feet. And on March 21, "Along time ago we dug a big under ground house and so today we put the roof on it now my brother is going to make one mine is about 3 feet deep and 5 feet across."

I remember that house, that cave, that trough in the hardpan of our backyard. I remember chipping away at the earth with the tip of a man-sized shovel that kept us busy for days. And after my brother's deep domain was hollowed out, I remember digging my own well in the earth a few feet from his. Then the great task was to cover both our troughs with any sheet or towel we could commandeer from the house, and then to dig a tunnel to crawl through from my brother's cave to mine. By the evidence of my brother's diary, the completion of this tunnel was a minor event: "We made a tunal and I went over to Hellens and Boppums house [our aunt and grandmother lived together nearby] to stay all night and they gave me a funny book."

In the eye of my memory, though, the tunnel was the great feature of the whole enterprise. So what if you could have a cave, with what we called the Indian blanket pitched over the top, suspended over a personal darkness with a couple of brooms? The real point was to have a place to go for help without being seen by surface-dwellers, or to share a snack smuggled underground, or just to crawl through on your belly, and then back again. The main thing was the connection.

According to Bret's faithful diary, we played horse and buggy with our wagon. Next day it was a rickshaw. Often, we went to Alum Rock Park, just east of town, to hike or have "a barb-aq." We took the wagon to school the day my brother could show the sixth grade (he was in third) his special edition of the *Weekly Reader* "in braial." We "made a boy club," and on TV at Grandma's we "watched Disneyland and it was about Indians." I gave my brother "a lot of bolders," and at Grandma's house we "made trails in the grass."

In those days, Bret was our historian: "We climbed eagle rock . . . ," he reports, and "I made a garden . . . I planted the seeds . . . we made a house with a blanket . . . we went to church . . . we saw a movie at school." He's on a good run, and the days are full of incidents, mostly sounding triumphant. Then, abruptly, the entries end while the days go on, date and blank, date and blank, until on the last page, he reports:

> June 13, I had to do lots of work
> June 14, school was out.

And that summer we moved north to Oregon.

Against the backdrop of these details, this series of discrete events recorded by my brother, I have a memory that holds a niche in his history. I remember one day at Alum Rock Park, east from San Jose, we two stood at the dark mouth of Joaquin Murrieta's cave. That bandit, they say, once hid his stolen gold in this cavern under the bay trees where quail called and my brother held my hand. We had to go in, I said. Maybe there was a coin or two that strayed. My brother demurred, but I pulled him in. He had to take care of me, could not let go. We groped with our feet, felt the damp breath of the dark. It was like being inside your own mind, making up the thoughts you could not see. Somewhere in that rich darkness, I knew, lay the bounty we deserved.

That's all I remember—not coming out, not what we may have found, not how far away our parents may have been, or what the girls were doing. I just remember going into the dark with my brother, connected by our hands.

Once, on a business trip after my brother was gone, I had a little free time in San Jose, and I found 3616 Kelso Court. It was maybe nine in the morning when I knocked, and a sleepy Hispanic gentleman in his pajamas opened the door.

"Sorry to bother you," I said, "but I used to live in this house—fifty years ago. Very sorry I woke you." He was rubbing his eyes.

"Take a look around, Señor," he said. "The house, the yard, anything."

I declined to step inside, but thanked him, and he closed the door. I tried the gate at the side. It swung open, and I stepped into the grand vista of that sun-bleached backyard yet remaining in my mind. Of course, in fact, it was cramped and fenced with solid boards on the three sides. Desperate grass tinged with brown struggled out of the hardpan soil. Crumpled paper from someone's birthday was stuffed into a trash bin, and a clothesline stretched from a hook by the back door to the dead stick that had once been an orange tree.

But in the far back corner, after half a century, I saw the two shallow depressions of our caves in the ground, with a little trench between them where our tunnel once had been. I looked down through time.

## BINOCULARS

What's in a name? There are millions: Joe, Sylvia, Mohamed. But one name is yours, and thus, when you are little, you are vulnerable. You can be crucified.

When we lived in San Jose, in 1957, we had a turtle the size of a silver dollar, a pet my brother named "Binoculars" or, as he spelled it in an early Mother's Day card, "Binokualars," for its little swiveling eyes. And I had a friend named Gary, the trusty renegade who took me shoplifting and taught me how to lie. Our school was named Loma Vista Elementary. I don't remember my teacher's name. But I do remember the rumor that the principal had a spanking machine in his office for kids like me.

Our parents had met in California, and maybe that's why in the circle of our traveling we had returned there. For a time, during the war, they lived in the mountains, up the Feather River, just north from the Gold Rush country of 1849. Our parents must have named my brother after the writer Bret Harte, of the California Gold Rush days. But in the 1950s, if you had that name it was only a matter of time before some bully on the playground got the notion to call out: "Hey, Brat! Is that your name, you little brat?" Not necessarily mean, you understand, but inventive—at a primitive level. Wordplay.

That had already happened, and my brother survived it. He told me one night, while we were about to fall asleep, "I just walked away, but it made me cry."

Then spring came. The days grew warm and school was a hazy progression of daydreams. One afternoon, at recess, my brother called to me from the hiding place in the laurel hedge above the playground. He stood among the dry leaves that had fallen and bent close to whisper.

"I thought of another name they could call me." He was still for a moment, breathless, holding the secret. I looked in his eyes. "Hair Barrette," he said.

"No one's going to call you that," I said.

"But they could," he said. "*I* thought of it."

A few months later, we moved north, to Oregon. Our father had a new job, and our mother wanted to get me away from Gary, the bad influence. I'm sure Gary was a minor factor, but that is how our mother explained the move to me. "We want you to be more like you really are."

Years later, after my brother had died, I found in a box of trinkets his miniature school dictionary from Loma Vista. As I flipped through the pages, I came to the word "turtle." And in the margin, in my brother's crooked scrawl, "I love you Binokualars."

## DOCTOR BRET

In Oregon, we were family friends with the Paulys. It was a given, as I have said, that my brother would marry Deborah, a few days younger than he. I would marry Deborah's younger sister, Becky. She suited me. Why not? And our sister Kit would marry Michael, the youngest in that parallel tribe.

Our two families would camp, walk the Oregon beaches, gather blackberries in August, and go to the mountains for a Christmas tree every December. Their father was from Austria, and the great moment of the year was when they lit real candles on their tree and we sang "Silent Night" together. You had to keep very still in that room while the candles burned. To stand up, to shift in place—even to raise your voice, it seemed to me—might swipe a candle flame, kindle fire, and set the tree, the house, our lives ablaze.

I remember the night long after, when I was home from college and our families were together for the evening, that I announced I was engaged. In a few months, I reported, I would be married to my redheaded girl from Fresno.

Becky cried out, "I don't want you to get married!" There was a moment of awkward silence. I realized in that silence it was not that she and I, or Bret and Deborah, or Kit and Michael ever might have wed. We were too much like siblings. By being the first to marry outside our circle, I had broken something. We would never be as we had been.

It wasn't until after my brother died that I learned a key moment I had not known from the early days. Deborah told me of an afternoon when she and Bret were left to play alone when very young. They played Doctor, examining each other closely, under, inside, the hidden. In the course of this exchange, Deborah spoke aloud what we all had thought true: "Do you think we might get married?"

Bret, maybe five, pulled back. "No," he said. "Not that. Never."

## WE'RE PALS

Our father's parents were far away. Earl had died before we were born, and Ruby was in Kansas, and soon she, too, was gone. But our mother's people were there. Grandma we called Boppums, unable in our first days to say her name of Lottie. And Grandpa Harrison was the kindly, giant former preacher with the biggest, softest hands you could ever hold.

One time, Grandpa had gifts for us. He gave me a hand-polished, dark steel pair of pliers that fit my fist perfectly. For my brother, he had some coins from Canada. Even then, I knew these gifts were wise. I tried to fix things with my hands. For my brother, vocation was more distant: repair of the world.

We were different, but we were pals. It's a caricature, perhaps, but I remember walking with our arms around each other's necks, chanting happily, "We're pals. We're pals. . . ." As I have said, we never fought. Hard to believe for our friends, but the most natural thing in the world for us.

Is that right? Is that best? What is the price of seamless calm? When I look back on the serene temperament we displayed, I wonder about the rare combination of pacifism, beauty, and silence that reigned between us. Can there be true kinship without conflict? We lived a code, seemed to possess a trick, sustained a magic calm.

Our mother now reports that once—once—Bret showed anger as a child. He had done something wrong and had been caught. When his behavior was being discussed, he suddenly shook off the armor of the good and shouted, "I hate you, Mama!"

At that time, she told me later, she thought to herself, "Yes, be more like that. Be bold, my son." But he was not so. Our world had come through war. Our family gospel was pacifism. How does a pacifist learn to live with anger, helpless frustration, the fury for self-preservation? How can a child negotiate pacifism as a principle of diplomacy between nations, and unremitting calm in the individual life?

Maybe my brother knew how to shout with others. I never heard him raise his voice at me. I did not know conflict with him. I think now how much he and I must have suppressed to keep the peace. Then, it was an idyll of right living. In the end, what did my pal carry, hidden from his best friend?

## THE WANDERER

In our family, among the four children, I held, from the beginning by our father's indulgence, a dispensation to wander. I had a pass to go beyond. "You know the road," he would say, giving me permission on family trips to rise early and walk the highway in the forward direction of our journey, to be picked up in due time, when the rest of the tribe came along in the car. When we camped, my custom was to rise in the dark and go scrambling up a ridge, along a river, somewhere away into my hidden distances by yearning and whim.

I remember once on Orcas Island, while everyone else had to break camp and pack, I walked forth along a country road. A storm was brewing, and the reeds twitched in the ditch. Wind whined in the phone lines overhead. I was striding into my vocation, chanting words, murmuring my yearning into syllables in tune with the moan and flail of the world.

I didn't wonder at this inequality: others doing chores, while my chore was to learn abroad, alone, in my intuitive explorations.

Years later, our mother told me about her first ramble in the woods with

Bill, shortly after their marriage. She had imagined going hand in hand along the trail on a romantic walk. But he left her, went scrambling up the ridge, calling over his shoulder that he would converge with her farther along. She trod the path alone, wondering what she had gotten herself into.

On Orcas Island that day, the road seemed to hum, and my feet caught the rhythm. The storm was seeking me, offering all it had to my open, welcoming heart. But back in camp, in the frenzy to gather all things before the storm hit, what was it like for Bret—the oldest, most reliable helper?

## WIZARD FALLS

My favorite place in the whole world: the Wizard Falls Trout Hatchery, beside the Metolius River, in central Oregon. Big pines, slow fragrant wind, and pool upon pool of beautiful fish.

Maybe eight years old, camped nearby with the family, I had been left to my own devices.

The sign said, "Do not touch the fish." But they were so beautiful, so big, so slow, turning in their pool, dappled rainbows heavy with the river's life. If I could touch one of those, I knew an electric vitality from the wild would thrill my body.

I would just touch one. Could that hurt? Kneeling by the pool, I watched for the right one. There she was. My hand went slowly through the reflection of my face on the shimmering surface of the pool. The great school turned in their spiral of abundance, and there was my one.

Just as my fingers touched the fish . . .

Wham! The ranger's hand grabbed my collar and jerked me to my feet.

"Don't let me ever see you here again!" His mouth was a frozen snarl.

*So what?*

So I slunk away, back to camp, said nothing of my disaster.

*So you had to leave?*

Well, yes, and it was my favorite place. Just when I did what I wanted, in that exact moment of my greatest wish, I was punished.

*So you were punished. So what?*

If you do what you want, you will be punished. That lesson went so deep, so often, I learned to not do what I want. Now it's hard to know what I want.

## TWO BIRDS WITH ONE STONE

The next year, Bret would be in junior high, but it was summer, and we went to explore the playground of his new school. Some big kids were playing hardball on the field above us. We skulked along below the bank. From the sky, the fly ball fell, striking my brother's head, and he began to cry. Then I began to cry. The face and lanky frame of a player appeared in silhouette above us.

"Looks like we hit two birds with one stone," he called over his shoulder to the others.

## STRAWBERRY FIELDS

Love, human love, was like two banks of a turning river. On one side, it was gentle, like shallow music. On the other, it was strident, like wrestling. At twelve, I stood on the bank with music, and looked across.

Jane Brown. I remember her name in red letters on small scraps of blue-lined paper, the confetti of my first love. It was school's last day, fifth grade. We were cleaning out our desks, choosing what to save, remember, or destroy. Jane Brown sat next to me, one row over—so well named, her hair the color of dark wood. She worked the flurry of her own chores. Her desk was neat inside. I saw, turning my head as if to look at the clock, or at Don sharpening his pencil, or at Bobbie, dipping for water at the fountain. Her desk was an open box with a stack of clean paper inside, and a pencil, sharp as a manicure, the eraser pink and never used. And a second pencil, red.

When we exchanged tests to check each other's spelling, she and I were partners. She wrote her name on my test, to show she had corrected it, and I wrote my name on hers, before we handed them back across the aisle. In my mind these tests were like love letters without a message, but with a name: at the top, my name, then a list of words, then her name below. And I had torn those names away to save them like coins, a miser of words, one name again and again in red.

She closed her desk with a tiny thump. I looked down at my fist. There she sat, here was her name in my hand, and the year was over.

That summer, I took a job in the strawberry fields. For once, my brother did not go with me. I had a job picking strawberries, the world of kid wage-earners in those old Oregon days. A bus picked you up from the corner down the street at dawn on a Saturday in June. It was a school bus, long and yellow, but inside was unlike anything I had ever known. The energy was electric, and sweetly profane. Some older kids did most of the talking. This wasn't a job for them. It was a reprieve.

We were dropped off somewhere out in the country, the field flat and the rows long. Dawn was biblical that morning. A gruff man instructed us to pick "Stems-on, don't eat no berries, and you don't get paid if the halleck's not full. And you're off the job if the berries is bruised." Then we were each directed to a row, the dewy leaves and crimson fruits bristling with promise, and we bent to our work as the sun began to climb.

The boss's rules were one thing, but I made a personal vow not to eat a single berry all day long. Puritan legacy from my family had trained me to restrain desire. I was a worker, after all, at last. Labor, and money, would be the transaction here. The bold bell of the rising sun rang in my eyes, blinding me, and forcing me to look down where dew feathered the strawberry leaves, and there—there in leaf shadow the primordial elegance of fat strawberries lolling, spilling, awaiting my hand. I picked feverishly, doing the math in my mind, and adding up my riches to be: a brave hoard of quarters, no doubt.

The big kids, when the old man's back was turned, hurled fat sappy ripe ones at each other. Even in my innocence, I knew this was something new. The boys hurled berries at the boys, and that was a dogfight. But when a girl hurled a berry at a boy, that was love.

Not so for me. I bent low in frenzy, nipping the stems with thumbnail on finger, and gentling the berries into the little veneer halleck box, fitting hallecks to the flat, and walking each completed flat to the weigh station, then back with an empty to my spot.

It is a brutal testament to my Brethren forebears that I made it through that day without once tasting sweet red flesh. The bus came, and we trailed our dusty way to meet it and settled in for the ride home. It was hot, and everyone was subdued, reduced to murmuring after the morning's shouts. As I leaned against the glass of the window, I secretly exulted: I had a job! I was out there!

Next day, as I bent to my row, I felt my virtue fray. I began to suffer attrition in my restraint. What did this life mean? What was pleasure for? A sentence appeared in my mind, pulsing in neon: "I'll just eat one."

There are many kinds of virginity—varieties of a great ending that coincide with a great beginning. The last time you believe everything your parents say . . . the last time you expect you will live forever . . . the last time you believe it is the job of someone else to make you happy. In an instant, once you choose, the old paradigm falls away, and you step into a brave new world. For me, the moment I offered that fat berry to my lips was such a choice. The taste of that long-denied Oregon strawberry given hot from the earth, biting back as I bit down with a tang of sweet reserved for the reticent—that was my welcome to direct experience in adult life. Part of me blossomed into the fullness of desire. Life would never be the same.

After that, I just ate one—at a time, now and again, and again, as I worked my way along the row. The flavor of that crimson sin seemed to waken me to what was happening around me. The older girls, and the one older boy, were speaking in code.

"Don't flip me the bone, you slut. I never did it with him once!"

It would be some years before I could translate that sentence, but it remained verbatim in memory until my mind was ready.

On the last day of that week of picking, I had my bag of quarters. I was rich. I was older. I was wise. The bigger kids had been spending time somewhere I couldn't see, especially the boy, Charlie, and the girl named Ramona. That last day, they two sat side by side in the last row as the bus pulled away. The sun sank low, and the bus rumbled along that dusty road. The kids around me all turned at once, their voices chattering like birds in a startled flock. Charlie and Ramona were locked in a kiss, their eyes closed, their hands holding what they could hold of each other—and all the shouting, all the catcalls, all the jive of insult masking our longing could not make them stop.

## FOUR

When I saw four mannequins in a store window once, I remember thinking, "That's as it should be." Four was my favorite number, the right number, the number of children in my family, and what was more bedrock than that? When I was four, I remember thinking this was the perfect age. And we didn't even have sister Barbara yet, so my interest in the number apparently goes deeper than I knew.

I was obsessed. I had read somewhere that in ancient times, some people thought four was the number of Earth (four seasons, four directions, four fingers—and that odd thumb—and so on). Three was the number of the spirit (father, son, and holy ghost). There were even monks who bragged about chewing each morsel of bread four times in honor of earth, and then taking three sips of wine in honor of the spirit. Or was it three for bread and four for wine? I can't remember. Anyway, numbers in those ancient days were not the zoo pets of math class—they ran the world.

And then, they said, those ancients realized that, hey, if you add four and three you get that weird, left-handed number seven (out of balance and magical—but musical, too: seven notes in the scale). And if you multiply four times three you get, wow—the number of disciples, the number (roughly) of full moons in a year (which really confirms this whole thing is cosmic), twelve days of Christmas. And a dozen doughnuts—no, that came later. But anyway, four is where everything starts, the foundation, before it gets all spiritual and strange. Four kids in a family, once Barb came along? We were the book of genesis.

As I did chores, under my breath I would count to four four times, and then do *that* four times, and *that* four times. Obsessive? Yes. Compulsive? Yes. OCD? Probably, though never diagnosed.

You just whisper under your breath, one two three four one two three four one two three four one two three four. . . . And then you do that again at a slightly different under-the-breath pitch so you know you are on that next cycle, and so on for the whole paper route, or round of dishwashing, or walk to school, or whatever other rhythmic eternity you find yourself trapped in.

I remember thinking, in those days of balanced fours, that if we were three, things would be out of kilter. We would be exiled from earth to the realm of spirit.

## MURDER BRIDGE

That's what our father called it—high and slender span over the deep gorge of the Crooked River south of Madras in central Oregon. Once when we were small, our family car rolled to a stop in the parking area at the south end of the crossing, and we all walked out onto the bridge to look down. It was beautiful in many ways, as the sight of distant water in dry country can be. That thread of silver and blue, way deep in the canyon's shadow, was a blessing.

Then Daddy was telling us a story. A woman had stopped here with her children, he said. They were being bad on the long drive. Maybe she was crazy, too, he said, but this is where she threw them over the edge and down.

"She's in prison now," he said. "That was a terrible thing."

I stood beside my brother, took his hand. Steady, now. We leaned, and together we looked over the barricade. In my mind I kept hearing the phrase "were being bad . . . were being bad . . ." and in my mind's eye the children were falling, flying, sprawled and getting smaller until they were gone into the blue shadow far below.

# BUYING FRI|OLES

Sometimes our parents had really good ideas—like taking us all out of school to drive to Mexico one spring. Our father had won some kind of big poetry award, and for the first time in our lives we actually had a new car—a big snow-white Oldsmobile station wagon. Our father drove, with our mother up front on the right, and baby Barbara between them. In back it was me on the left, sister Kit in the middle, and Bret on the right. We drove long and fast, deep into the far land. We watched a labor parade in Hermosillo, saw alligators up a little river from San Blas, climbed the pyramids at Teotihuacán. In a library at Guanajuato I spent long afternoons writing my school paper on Mexican music.

My brother's take-along homework was mostly math. He was way beyond me at that point. One problem on the list required him to find a pound of beans, do some kind of numerical estimation, then count. So the two of us set out to find the beans.

We walked along narrow streets in the old town—was it San Miguel? I can't remember. But I do remember trying to figure out what kind of shop would have beans, and asking for help of an old woman on the street.

"Beans?"

"Bee-yens?"

My brother made a folded tortilla shape with his left hand, and with his right he scooped invisible beans into his mouth. I was impressed.

"Ah! Frijoles! Sí. Allá." She pointed to a door, turned, and went her way.

My brother turned the knob, and we were inside. No one seemed to be at the counter, so we approached, and my brother cleared his throat. Through a beaded curtain behind the counter two girls emerged, about our age.

"Buenos días, muchachos—señores," said the older one.

"Um, buenos días," my brother said. "We need fri-ho-lays."

"Frijoles?" This struck them as hilarious, and they covered their mouths and laughed. My brother turned red, and so did I.

"How—much?" said the older girl, getting control of herself. "How much—frijoles—you want?"

"Um, a pound."

"Po-yund?" They laughed again, their long braids flying as they whirled this way and that.

My brother cupped his hands, and the girl looked over the counter into the shape he made, then looked in his eyes.

"Bueno," she said, looking down.

There was some kind of electricity in the air I didn't understand, like just after lightning, or just before. The air seemed to brighten from somewhere. There was a moment when everything was very still, my brother bowed over his cupped hands, and the girl, just for a moment, bowed before him.

## SHOOTING MY BROTHER

In third grade, I dropped down to the lower reading group. Since our mother was teaching at my school—a different class, but in close monitoring position—this was a big deal. She had already suffered terribly during the head-lice, child-by-child inspection, when the principal had reported to her that I had the dirtiest head in the school. I heard plenty about that. That was bad. But to be an iffy reader—this was a disaster.

Various remedies were tried, but none could budge me from the low group. My reading was slow, labored, subject to easy distraction. Finally, in desperation, our father made, for a pacifist, a strange offer: "If you can get into the higher reading group, we'll get you a gun—the kind that shoots real bullets."

This bribe, counter to all the child-rearing books our parents followed—had an immediate effect. I applied myself, moved up, and got the gun.

It was a beauty, a pump-action pellet gun that shot little lead slugs that you could bury deep in the bark of a tree if you pumped five times (two more than the manual suggested). The stock was real wood—probably pine, but stained like walnut. Gun-metal barrel and trigger. Bolt-action chamber where you dropped the pea-sized bullet. Now I was ready to survive anything.

After that, the gun was my constant companion in the woods below our house. When we played war, or mountain men and Indians, or the "Swamp Fox" from a TV show then popular, others had to use sticks for pretend guns, but my gun, unloaded, of course—of course—was real pretend.

I can't remember exactly how it happened, but I do remember adrenalin was high that day. We were three on a side, and my side had their side on the run. Did I happen to have a pellet in the chamber, and the gun pumped up—and forget it was in there? Or did I stop in the heat of the chase, and load up? All I remember is the blur of my brother running downhill through the ferns and my gun following to get a bead on his back, and then the awful magic of the trigger, and the bullet was on its way.

How I longed to bring it back, would have bled to pull that bullet back into the gun, as if I could see the tapered gray streak of my sin spiraling toward my Bret.

It missed him. Thank God I was a terrible shot, and the pellet thudded into an alder tree. But the look on his face when he turned, the game gone from the woods, the pellet embedded in the tree beside him, and his eyes, from twenty yards away, drilling into mine.

I promised to never do that, anything like that, again. And he never told. The other kids made me feel it, and I left the gun at home for a time. But the parents never knew what I had done, what kind of boy I had become. What kind of brother.

## SMOKING LEAVES

In our town, when we were down by the lake, where the rich kids lived, we could see their speedboats carving wakes, dragging skiers, throttling down as they coasted toward docks their mansions owned. But there was this one place where we could approach the water, where the railroad tracks cut through our town and even the rich people couldn't fence off their playground.

I was kneeling down picking up cigarette butts, the ones that still had a nub of tobacco left beyond the filter.

"You're not going to smoke those, are you?" my brother said.

I shook my head but kept gathering. In my mind, I was working it out like this: "No, I'm not going to smoke these. . . . I'll take the tobacco from them and pack it into the pipe I made from an elderberry stem, and smoke that!"

Some days later, after school, I was in my secret den under the cedar stump down in the woods below our house, stuffing tobacco into my elderberry pipe. I lit it, took an exploratory draw, choked as the smoke bit my throat, gagged, then puffed in reverse, blowing smoke out through the lit pipe. My pleasure was transgression, a tangy sensation I believed my brother would never know.

## BALL OF FIRE

We came up through Texas out of Mexico the summer of my seventh-grade year, bound for our father's heritage home in Kansas. Hot, long miles. My appointed station was the left-hand window of the back seat, and the car was listing somewhat in my direction, because of the heap of rocks I had collected at my feet. When our father had noticed this effect somewhere in Michoacán, he decreed that for every new rock I picked up, I had to discard two. I neatly solved this legislation in my favor by picking up boulders and discarding pebbles.

At the end of a long day, we made it to Junction City, Kansas, to stay with our father's sister Peg and her husband, Bill. While the family inhaled lemonade in the kitchen, Bill, a retired newspaperman, dozed in front of the television. Peg warned us not to switch off the TV.

"If you leave it on, he sleeps. If you turn it off, he wakes up, and none too happy."

That night we kids were arrayed, as per our traveling custom, in a row of four sleeping bags on the floor of the living room. We were beat, the room was stuffy, and we slept in our underwear. It had been a long day, and everyone went down at once.

Sometime in the night, I woke to the sound of distant thunder. It seemed to come up through the ground to tickle me, and I thought: what would it be like to see that storm from the top of the hill?

With stealth long practiced in my life as a secret Indian, I rose from the row of sleepers and padded, shoes and pants in hand, to the door. Once I had eased the screen back snug, I dressed and set out up the street toward the highest place. In about five blocks, I came to the opening—a twisted oak on a knoll with a panoramic view of dusky wheat fields far to the west, and yes! A shot of lightning lit a little spot of gold halfway to the horizon.

I settled on the ground, my back against the tree, to watch the show. Best I ever saw, the lightning stepping closer, each jag lighting a wider sphere of beauty, thunder crawling across the earth and into me.

It keeps happening in my life—these times when terror and beauty and stern learning knot into a single moment. The obvious fact that one does not sit under a lone tree on a hilltop in a lightning storm—this arrived in my mind together with the overhead bolt that sizzled close as the ozone smoke I gasped, and left a ball of fire hovering before me, swaying and slowly approaching my naked mind.

Rain thundered where running I collapsed into the gutter, my hand inside my mouth in terror, and water rushing at my back. But the ball of fire had vanished, and as I stood to run any direction down, my heart thrilled for what I had survived—seen, been in, and lived beyond.

It took me some time to find the house. I wrung the water from my pants, left my sopping shoes by the car, and teased open the screen and went inside. Four sleeping bags, three lumps of life on the floor. And on the couch, with the lamp turned low, our father was writing, as was his custom. Mildly, he looked in my direction.

"You're wet," he whispered.

"Yeah," I said. "The storm."

I crawled into my bag and lay still. Our father never asked. And unto my brother, I never said a word.

What had gone from us, that I kept silent then? We had turned out of the two-rutted road we had long walked together, onto diverging trails.

## UNCLE MILEY

When you are young, the big people tell all kinds of stories—about their own childhoods, about friends we knew, and others we would never meet, about relatives near and far. And there are certain stories that are told as parables, nuggets of mystery, where the important part is what is not said. Plenty of those with our clan. And then there are the stories that are not told at all—to you. There are secrets, and then there are secrets told secretly.

Among these for me was the tale of Uncle Miley, a brother-in-law back on the Nebraska prairie in the era of horses. I heard this story with my ear to the upstairs heat vent at a neighbor's house, one Saturday afternoon, when it was too rainy to play outside. The big people were downstairs talking among themselves in the kitchen, and the kids safely gone, upstairs—my brother and sisters and I. I don't remember what the other kids were doing up there, somewhere in another room, but I lay on the floor with my ear to the grate, where it led down some shaft through the walls, to listen to big people talk.

"It was so strange," said my Aunt Helen, our mother's sister, "the way Miley disappeared. I was just a child, and didn't really know much about it. They said they found his buggy by the river, the horse left in harness there, at dusk. And no sign of Miley at all. It was the first time I heard that mysterious phrase, when they talked about it: 'Foul play was suspected.' Foul play. What an idea."

I heard a muffled reply, a question.

"Well," said Helen, "his wife and the three girls moved in with us. It was wonderful, really. Here I had three new sisters to play with—Evelyn, Marion, and Grace. We had the best time, the four of us girls, and two mothers. We were too many to keep track of, and the mothers had each other. But then that, too, came to an end.

"It was Valentine's Day. All the kids were up making valentines, working around on the upstairs floor. I was by the heat vent from the kitchen downstairs. I heard my aunt's voice, talking with Mother. Something was wrong, I could tell that. We all hushed and gathered around the vent to listen. Pretty soon, in all their fast whispering down below, we heard the word 'Miley,' and then 'home,' and then they were quiet. Then there was some more whispering, and the deeper sound of Daddy's voice.

"Pretty soon we heard the stairs creak, and we scattered out again, to work on our valentines. My aunt came in, pale, with a letter in her hand. We kids all looked up, but she didn't say anything for a moment. Then, 'Miley's coming back,' she said. That sentence scared us cold. We thought Miley was dead. 'He's coming back from Idaho,' she said. 'From Idaho.' And the letter kind of trembled in her hand.

"So he came home, on the train. The menfolk went to the station to get him. I lost my three sisters. They went back to the old place. People acted strangely. Were they happy he was back? I couldn't tell. And why had he left? Was life just too much for him? That's no way to do—just to leave. And to leave the horse like that, in harness . . .

"Miley was fixing up their old place, that summer. He was up on the roof, repairing the shingles, when he was struck by lightning and killed. And after that, we moved away, and everything sort of came apart.

"But I never did learn why he went away. Or why he came back. He was a dreamy character, like someone in a play who exits, and then later he enters again, and then he exits a last time."

There was a pause, some muffled words.

"Well," someone said, "we'd better see what the kids are doing."

## ROUNDS

In our garage there was a workbench with a vise and grindstone, and an array of hand tools, each with a story of origin somewhere back in the family lore. This hatchet from C.O. camp . . . this hammer hafted with hickory from Kansas . . . this pruning knife with the rosewood handle from the orchard called Yaggy in our father's early days.

The workshop was my realm of obsession. So many things in my life I could not make happen. School was a struggle, homework often dreary, and friends hard to find. I had a brother, after all, if I needed companionship. But often, I wanted to be alone. So I made things in the garage.

Now and then one of these enigmas will appear from our mother's attic, or a box from the back room. There is the cricket cage glued together from bamboo splints. The complete set of miniature Indian weapons fashioned of filed nails, red thread, and split bamboo. Whittled oak head the size of a golf ball, with eyes of mussel shell. The club of locust wood, inset with a sharpened stone, and finished with a squirrel tail hung from a braided string. And now and then, some remnant of the jewelry collections of polished date seeds and ground coconut shell.

Our father had passed along a book to me about that time called *Two Little Savages*, by Ernest Thompson Seton. This book led me further, to Seton's *Wild Animals I Have Known*, and then *Rolf in the Woods*, and others. The books were filled with accounts of boys and even grown men who spent their time whittling, trapping, hunting, making a tepee and being Indians. There was something like religion in all this for our father. Utter independence from the restraints of modern life resided in such practices of survival in the wild, living by one's wits, old ways of being on the earth, prior to all polite behavior. When our father talked to me, through these books, his sermon was all about being wild—or as he sometimes said, "friendly, but not tame."

Somehow, I became the Indian of the family. My brother was the reader, the historian, the good student. He studied Indians; I decided to be one. So I worked with my hands, and gradually, our father's tools became mine.

Years later, when I spent a summer at a remote station in Alaska, I reported in a letter home my memory of these early crafts: "At home when I start some little craftsie thing I get it started and get all excited about how neat it's going to be and how well someone will like it and before I get all discouraged by my lack of talent I am sidetracked by something else, I put the half-way project down, it sifts to the bottom of my drawer never to be seen again, and I am still confident that I could have made it great."

Somehow the actual failure of the object would not dim my enthusiasm for making. There was some kind of magic in this process, for even failure produced materials for a story. As a college student on that summer job in Alaska, I was still playing at capricious creation. My partner on the remote hill station, Wendall, observed that I was the "jack of all futile attempts, master of none." As I reported by letter:

> I carved a little bear that was ok so I gave it to W. for his birthday. But then I tried a dancing bear that was changed to a leopard half way through but ended up looking like a crippled bulldog. My reclining man was a real creep, and sitting boy with flowers looks like a piece of mud and the flowers broke off. So I switched to metal work. I carefully shaped a piece of wire with a hammer and tongs; curved it to a perfect circle; filed and sanded it much to the discomfort of my fingers, and slipped the gleaming bracelet onto my arm: a smashed up piece of wire still, and I threw it away.
>
> Next, basketweaving: it looked like an old bird's nest. So: painting. I didn't have any water colors so I remembered tempera is made with egg yolks and frescoes were made with egg whites. So I whipped up a batch of each, made some brushes, tossed in a little dirt and such for color, and slapped it on a board. I don't have to tell you. Scrambled eggs, on a board.

Back home in childhood, what was Bret doing all that time I was drilling tiny holes for date seeds to be earrings? What were his obsessions while I knapped obsidian with a sharpened deer bone on a scrap of leather against my palm? And the real question, the strange one: Why don't I know? Where was my pal?

One of the chores for Bret and me was to mow the lawn with the push mower. We did this festive chore by taking turns, round by round. Zest was the musical key—to start your round with a sprint, bank the turns with balletic style, and race into the homestretch for the hand-off. The goal was to time this exchange so that the mower never stopped.

This sense of team rhythm was exercised in several projects around the homestead—digging, raking, picking up cones of the Douglas fir, shoveling snow. Our greatest chore was to be the building of a deck behind the house, to surround the tulip tree our parents had planted years before. The design was given, boards bought, nails boxed, foundation beams placed by our father, and hammers handed out. Then our father disappeared.

I remember the percussive hours of pounding nail after nail, a pair of sinkers side by side each time the two-by-four would cross the four-by-six beam.

This had been going on for several summer days when I looked up to fetch more nails and Bret was gone. I checked the house, our room. Empty.

When I found him, he was behind the raspberry hedge, holding his right forearm in his left hand. I could tell he had been crying.

"Look at my arm," he said. "It's all swollen."

"Are you okay?" I said. His right arm was bigger, yes.

He looked at the ground, then at me. "I can't pound like you," he said. "You're better at it."

I put my arm around his shoulders. This first time, he did not return the gesture. My pal just stood there, and eventually I led him back to the house.

"Let's take a break," I said. "No hurry."

## PROUD OF HER PROW

There was a big kid in our neighborhood, Roger, who had a paper route and seemed to have money to burn. Actually, he had two—the Big Route, south of A Avenue, and the Little Route, on our side of A. As Roger got farther into high school, his route started impinging on his social life, so he recruited my brother and me to be his substitutes. When he had something coming up, he would give us a call in the evening, and we would cover for him the next day after school.

My brother insisted on taking the big route, farther from our house. And he insisted we be paid equally, in spite of his longer labor. There were some matters where he could prevail, being the older one—and hey, it worked for me.

The routine went like this: you slung the canvas bag over the back rack on your bike, and headed down to the corner of Tenth and A, and there beside the Episcopal Church was a drop box, painted yellow, where the papers would be deposited for the carriers, stacks bound in cotton string. You cut the string, counted out your number, filled your bag, and set out. Several other routes departed from this box, and there were generally two or three others boys counting out their own sets of papers when we arrived.

One day, when we got to the drop box, the other carriers weren't counting papers but silently kneeling in the shade of a low-hanging cedar. We stepped up and looked over their shoulders, and there she was, Playmate of the Month. I don't remember her name, or the pose, exactly, for she shimmered before my eyes like a glance into the sun. But I do remember the caption: "Proud of Her Prow." And quite a prow it was.

I know in some families the father shows the boy such things, or the older brother shows the younger. Or a friend shows a friend. For us, it was otherwise. We came upon this forbidden wonder together, marveled in silence, and never spoke of such things after.

Dreams came, the kind that woke me wet. I began to understand lines in songs that had passed me by: "The dizzy dancing way you feel." The family album of *Great Paintings in the Western Tradition* turned out to include Thomas Hart Benton's *Persephone*, with her scarlet robe unfurled. And once, when we stayed with family friends at the coast, I noticed a magazine in a stack by the fire, rose in the night and took it out the door, down the lane, to a streetlight to gaze at the infinite promise of a girl dressed in a hammock and a smile.

Of the accumulating silences between my brother and me, this one about women, beauty, passion, sex—this marked a boundary between us. We shared a room, and a life as almost twins. But here we parted ways in silence.

## LES MISÉRABLES

When my brother was first learning to type, he began a letter to President Kennedy, "As a fourteen-year-old and as an American, I commend your attitude toward world peace and a ditching of the Cold War for a line of peace in a world which has never been in need of it more." His was a voice from a very early age for leadership in the fair treatment of misunderstood people far away. The beauty of this approach was that it called forth the fullness of one's idealistic soul; the difficulty was that a sense of advance in the direction of your aspirations was elusive in the extreme.

About the same time, he had the misfortune to read Victor Hugo's novel *Les Misérables* in its entirety. I don't remember how this happened, but the effect was immediate: the sorrows of the world yawned open, and my brother took charge of them.

As Christmas approached, one evening we were discussing what we might get. What we might want.

"I don't want anything," my brother said to the family. "Use the money you might have spent and give it to the U.N."

"What?" I said.

"It's not necessary to have anything," he said, "when so many do not."

The Christmas morning that followed was a haunting spectacle. In my customary frenzy to tear paper away and see what I got, I would look up at my brother sitting still, watching. "That's nice," he said, as I pulled out my model kit for the battleship *Conestoga*.

This approach to leveraging world salvation on the fulcrum of the denied self was somewhat familiar to me from family custom. We had each week what we called "Sacrifice Meal," when we ate only cornbread and milk for dinner, and each put money in a bowl for the needy.

But my brother's self-denial was extreme, even in such a family as the Staffords. I began my own note to Santa that year (preserved with other scriptures in a box in the attic), with a goody-goody preamble:

> Dear Santa: For Xmas I guess it's for you to decide whether I get any presents—one thing you might want to give me a little early is a few ideas on what others want so I can do the funnest thing in the world, giving.

Then I concluded with my transparent, conflicting wishes: "I would like a model of a dog that I saw in a store and of course anything (as long as it isn't girls' stuff) that you are going to throw away." In that, I believe I spoke the puritan's hypocritical party line. But my brother's self-denial was real. He began then, it seems to me, to starve himself, like Mother Shipton in the Bret Harte story "The Outcasts of Poker Flat." She ate nothing so others might live. And my brother, at twelve, as he told us his resolve, had started on a path of denial. By denying his own wishes, he thought he fed others. No one seemed to object to this twist on the family's modest ways.

Years later, in school, we read Dickens's *Tale of Two Cities*. When the novel's martyr speaks his last lines, I thought of my brother:

> It is a far, far better thing that I do, than I have ever done; it is a far, far better rest that I go to, than I have ever known.

## SWEET LITTLE GUN

Our father had a .22 pistol I loved: steel tinged with blue, and you could unscrew the barrel, hold it up to the light, and savor the spiral grooves of the rifling that would guide the slug, spin it straight and true. The brass shells fit so snug in their chambers, and the grip was cross-hatched, fine as a fingerprint.

Sometimes our father would let us shoot this little beauty. It seemed a friendly toy to me, not a weapon. It was an implement to knock a beer can off a stump in the Sand Hills of Kansas, not an instrument of death.

When I look back now and see our father's hands lovingly holding it out, grip first, to me, to my brother, to our sisters, it was his childhood he was giving us, his time of freedom on the prairies of Kansas, in the 1930s, when you hunted food for the family—rabbits and squirrels and quail—and there would never be another war.

"We'll stand here behind you," he would say. "Hold it steady. See that cottonwood leaf on the bank? Erase that leaf!"

## 1909-s

We collected stamps, with an album each, and periodic trips to the stamp store downtown. We steamed commemoratives off letters from our father's office—even some foreign correspondence. And we traded duplicates when we were in the mood.

Then it was coins, begun when our parents took us all to Britain. It was a literary tour for our father (he stood in silence at Southey's grave in Grasmere), but for the rest of us it was simple rambling. We traveled without a car, and the custom was to go by train to the next place that tempted us. The folks would leave us four kids at the station with the luggage, and they two would go in search of lodgings. Sometimes they were gone a long time. We had been raised with the motto, "Don't forget to talk to strangers," so we were never at a loss if need arose—directions to a nearby sweet shop, "Milk Bar," or park. Then the folks would return, and we would portage our things to whatever obscure B&B they had found for us.

In the prelude to this journey, while we traveled across the USA for our flight from New York, I had found an arrowhead beside the road in Iowa. When our crusty landlord in Edinburgh expressed an interest in "Red Indians," I gave him the point. Delighted, he gave us each a big old English penny from Victoria's reign, and my brother and I caught the fever. The old pennies were still in circulation in 1961, and we soon had a shoe-box full.

Collecting mania had us in thrall, and when we tramped the open country east of Edinburgh called King Arthur's Seat, we began to find first bullets from a former shooting range, then a few round musket balls from earlier days, and finally—a great coup—a dingy green piece of metal in an odd shape we felt required a trip to the Royal Museum of Scottish Antiquities. The indulgent curator, summoned from his office by our parents, turned the thumb-sized implement in his hands.

"By Jove," he said, "it's Bronze Age." We had found a socketed axhead, circa 1000 B.C.

"What should we do with such a thing?" I asked.

"Some chaps," he replied, "might donate it to a museum—this one, for example."

Done.

Back home in Oregon, Bret and I began a collection of American pennies together, revved by the almost daily thrill of contributing a missing penny to the three-panel array of the twentieth century. For each year, each mint, you pried out a pasteboard disk from the case, and pressed the penny in where it belonged. Indian Heads from the real old days? Fantastic. Those zinc oddities from the war years? Stupendous. We got our trove from rolls of pennies traded for dollars at the bank, from family change, and from the street—how eagle were our eyes. And now and then, at the coin shop downtown, we would pore over values of the rare.

The most rare of all, as I remember, was the 1909-s VDB. Did "S" stand for the San Francisco mint (as "D" for the Denver)? That's how I remember it. But "VDB"? I learned later these were the initials of the designer, and partway through the mint run, the initials were removed, resulting in rarity for the coins so marked.

What followed was one of my brother's most precious, but short-lived, transgressions of our code. Visiting our neighbor Bobbie, Bret spotted a 1909-s penny in the neglected slush pile of Bobbie's own, more casual collection. This fired his soul. Masking his excitement, my brother casually traded Bobbie for the penny, offering more worth than Bobbie expected, but far below market value for the coin. Then, when Bret got home, he mentioned to me that he had decided to start his own penny collection.

"Ours is mostly done," he said to me. "And we'll keep working on that. But I want to start over, and just make my own." Sounded fine to me.

But somehow, our father caught wind of this plot. Maybe Bret, with rare pride, showed him the penny. The boom came down. Not only was Bret's new collection nixed, but Bret was dispatched to Bobbie's house to return the penny and apologize.

"You can't take advantage of people like that," our father said. "Especially a friend."

So Bret didn't get his own collection, and he lost his treasure, and our common collection, along with my brother's rare selfish verve, faded into oblivion.

The last day we had been in Edinburgh, Bret and I took a dash to the slope beyond our previous exploring at King Arthur's Seat. It was a tall steep of heather that fell away on the north to a narrow road below. We were in high spirits, feeling our freedom, farther from the family than we ever were allowed. The clouds hung low, the day was growing dim, and we were expected back at the B&B.

It must have been my suggestion, as the bad boy of the family, to pry a boulder from the hill, and see how far it might roll. We tried a little one, got our four hands behind it, tipped it up, and let it go. It bounded down the hill as if we had brought stone to life, and took a wild leap over the road, to disappear in fern far below. How satisfying!

"One more," I said. "Just one."

"My brother scanned the road. No car. "Okay," he said. "One."

I chose a huge one, perched on a little ledge screened by rowan scurf gnawed low by wind. It took all we had to lift this beauty from her fit, but when we had it teetering, braced against our knees, we saw there was a book pressed into earth beneath it. What could that be? Bronze Age metal was one thing—but a hidden human secret quite another.

There was a wild dance among us all—the stone just in balance at our knees, our four hands scooping up the damp book, the wind twitching at its leaves as they came open. And then the stone began to roll, a car appeared around the bend below, from our four hands the pages of some dark story exploding in a sudden buffet of wind, secrets flying over the moor as the boulder ran for the road and the car, and my brother and I, utterly of one mind, fled gasping over the hill.

## TRICK OR TREAT FOR UNICEF

When we were very small, our parents took my brother and me for a kind of Halloween I have never heard of since. Our mother made cookies, and we would approach a house in costume (me Daniel Boone, my brother George Washington) and knock.

When the door opened, instead of saying "Trick or Treat," we would say "Happy Halloween" and hold out the plate of cookies. We were not to take anything. We were to offer.

At one house, I remember, there was a big party going on inside. We could hear shouts and music. When the door opened, there was a very tall Ichabod Crane with a pumpkin for a head.

"Good evening," he said, and lifted off the head. We ran in terror, cookies scattered in our wake.

In junior high we updated the generous twist on Halloween by going house to house, dressed in our best school clothes, with a tin can.

"Happy Halloween," we would say and hold out the cup. "Trick or Treat for UNICEF."

Most people didn't get it. We had to explain that they were supposed to give us money, which we would pass along to the United Nations Children's Fund.

What came, often, was a dribble of pennies or a single dime. I remember the last house in my UNICEF career, the one that convinced me to move on to other forms of good behavior. The man who opened the door was dressed in loose trousers and a greasy T-shirt. He was holding a can of beer.

"Happy Halloween. . . . Trick or Treat for UNICEF."

"What the hell?"

We stared at each other for a moment.

"Sorry to disturb you, sir." I said. I turned and was gone.

## CALCULUS

Junior high—what can I say? Hormones burn like rocket fuel, but the rocket of the body is chained to earth. I remember our teachers struggling to maintain their dignity, their sanity, as we staged an ongoing medieval torture regimen for them.

Miss Peetz, discovered smoking in the closet of her classroom before school.

Mr. Lomax, breaking the snare drum as he demonstrated a fury of sound.

Mr. Sullivan, confessing to us, when cornered, that he could not think about atomic weapons or he would go mad.

Mr. Seeger, whipping out a knife when he felt threatened by the big boys on the wrestling mat—his last day on the job.

But me? I was on my best behavior. Note to parents: "Kim certainly should be commended for his classroom behavior and his fine attitude toward school." Our mother kept that note.

Why do certain little things remain tenaciously in mind? In grade eight, I was struggling with a math problem: how many times 19 goes into 57.

The problem strikes me now as about fourth-grade level. But that was my problem, and I was stalled. As others worked in silence, I approached the desk of our kindly teacher, Mrs. Williams.

"I can't get this," I said, showing her my page. "I tried 2, and that doesn't work. I tried 4, and that doesn't work."

She looked at me with almost-contained amusement. "Try 3," she said.

I returned to my desk, and *voilà!* It worked.

This memory makes what follows deeply mysterious. Mrs. Williams suggested I take the test for placement in the advanced math group. By some deep flaw in the assessment system, I passed. Worst of all possible outcomes: I was in advanced math all through high school. Completely out of my depth, faking it with the best of them.

The one benefit of this arrangement: for four years I studied mathematics with my brother, and we battled the beast together.

My first year at this lofty endeavor was in a class taught by Mr. Burt, whose priority seemed to be not New Math but leatherwork. Now here was a kindred soul. When you came into his classroom, you found him stitching together a sheepskin hat or a pair of moccasins. He asked his students to bring in their spent toothpaste tubes so he could melt them down for the tin he needed to get the alloy right and mold bullets for his muzzleloader. At least that's how I remember the plan.

The math was a different matter because of a provocative coincidence. There was another Kim in class, and she was cute, helplessly flirty, and on the rally squad—strutting and dancing at games for the Lake Oswego Sailors. She often wore her short-skirted Sailors outfit to school. When Mr. Burt described a problem in some detail and called out, "Kim, go to the board and solve this for us," several things happened in quick succession. For some reason, maybe it was that cute Kim, I was daily stricken with evidence of my advancing puberty, and the adjustments required to stand quickly and go to the board—with my back to the class, please!—took finesse. If cute Kim stood and flounced, my physical difficulty increased. If I stood first, all eyes were on me, and I had no time for adjustments.

That's basically what I remember of Algebra I.

By the next year, I was across the street at the high school, at the back of the room where Mr. Watkins was generally unable to attain accuracy with thrown chalk for the slackers, and where I could hunch down and make notes about what to ask my brother when we did our homework together that night.

I should say that my brother and I had a code, a musical way to be together. After watching a few episodes of *Zorro* on TV, we took a liking to the minor character named Señor Mendoza. We started calling each other Señor Mendoza, or simply Señor.

> Say, Señor Mendoza, did you get the problem set for tonight?
> Let me check, Señor. . . .

Somehow this name evolved into Señor Mendelphoze, perhaps influenced by our study of Gregor Mendel in the genetics unit in Mr. Hopper's biology class.

> Mendelphoze, Daddy says mow the lawn.
> Señor, I've got first round on you.

Given this habit for patois known only to us and a need to conquer the mysteries of higher mathematics on deadline, our homework routine became one of my purest memories of my brother. If I could sneak back through time to witness one dimension of our affection for each other, it would be this.

We would be in our room, each at a desk. The radio was on. The smell of dinner wafted down the hall. Time was short and we were in this together.

As we began to take the night's problems one by one, first we talked, pausing to savor a particularly beautiful pop chorus from the radio, or a particularly mysterious feature of the problem at hand, and then we forged ahead. But soon—how can I describe this?—we began to sing. Our voices wove together details of the math problem, morsels of encouragement, a wacky snatch about anything that rhymed with phrases from the radio, fragments from recent jokes, and, when necessary, rhythmic nonsense.

Can I do it now, calling out to you, my brother?

> Take the sine, cosine by a factor of two,
> Something like that square root two—
> Just one problem, nineteen more,

> Watkins wants an even score—
> Baby uum, uum, Baby uum. . . .

We jived equations to "Will I be pretty, will I be rich? Que será, será." We reduced the function of $x$ to "Listen to the rhythm of the falling rain." And most memorably, we encountered any problem without fear after "Tell Laura that I love her. . . ."

> As they pulled him from the twisted wreck
> With his dying breath they heard him say. . . .

And we said it, sang it loud, loved it in unison: "Tell Laura that I love her. . . . Tell Laura that I need her. . . . Tell Laura not to cry. . . . My love for her will never die. . . ."

As scholars, we faltered year after year. I felt compassion for Mr. Watkins but could not help his anguish by improved performance, no matter how hard I tried. Without each other, this might have been a failure. But together we sailed serenely through it all.

Our twin career in higher math flamed out in college, when we took a calculus class together from the daunting Dr. Ghent. I squeaked by with a C, and Bret took the F—a badge of courage, in my eyes, a great accomplishment.

And that was the end of the singing homework duo, *Los dos señores*, K + B.

## CREVASSE

When we were Boy Scouts, my brother and I were among "the older boys" with special dispensation to stray beyond. We were the ones who went ahead along the trail and, with practiced knuckle and palm, printed "bear tracks" across the path, then dawdled until the rest of the troop caught up, and asked our scoutmaster about them, and savored his extended discussion of safety, the "buddy system," and personal hunting exploits. We were the ones who set up distractions for our leader so the other boys could slip stones into his pack, one at each stop for rest, to slow him, and give us all reprieve from forced march, frequent rests, and the pleasure of his volcanic laugh when he opened his pack in camp. We were the ones who almost managed to launch the smallest boy among us into flight, tied to a twenty-foot pine sapling bent to earth.

In camp at our favorite place of all, Jefferson Meadows, high in the central Oregon Cascades, we ate from boxes of primitive Bernard's dehydrated food wrapped in paper-backed foil, swam naked in the lake, waged a losing battle against clouds of mosquitoes, practiced knot-work, held compass contests, performed Morse code mirror-flashing, created first-aid plans for the macabre scenarios invented by our scoutmaster, and survived other episodes in learning to be soldierly men.

One morning, my brother and I got to looking up at the mountain where it rose abruptly from the meadows surrounding our camp. What was it like up there? How high could you go? What dangers and wonders lurked far above the trail?

Somehow we convinced our scoutmaster, a benign miniature Marine, to let us find out, just the two of us, if we promised to "rope up" and proceed with care. It seems fantastic now that he gave permission. We knew nothing, really, about the mountains.

We scrambled up a forested ridge to where the trees were twisted by wind and shattered by avalanche. Then we stepped out onto the glacier. We donned the flimsy snow goggles we had made of foil from the food packets, with slits cut Eskimo-style to block the splendor of the sun on ice. And we had a ten-foot length of manila line tied with a bowline knot around my brother's waist and a matching bowline around mine.

My brother went first. We had discussed the danger of the hidden crevasse, fueled by a rumor we had heard from some nature show the other boys had watched. My brother took a boulder about the size of his head and flung in violently onto the glacier before him. When no crevasse opened, he stepped forward, picked up the stone, and flung it down again, like a cartoon figure, repetitive. I brought up the rear, and thus we made our halting, staggering, Sisyphean way across the white blank steep.

We climbed until we could no longer see the camp or the ant-boys far below. We climbed until we had found ribbons of ice in a hue of blue we had never known. The air was ethereal, and we had returned to some pure form of boy, unencumbered by effort beyond the physical, pleasure in seeing, in being, in ascending as two in one. There was a kind of light up there I have not seen anywhere else. The light was so clear that the image of my brother, stepping doggedly ahead of me, could not be tarnished by time. It was a visual effect that my field guide to weather describes as "Not rare, but rarely seen."

We climbed until my brother's arms began to shake, lifting the stone. He looked back at me, the stone in his gloved hands. I remember teetering on the brilliant slope, our bodies steaming, my brother's face shining with sweat, and with a fire from within.

"Señor," he said.

Not a question. A connection. The rope lay still on the snow between us. For a few moments we stood, not speaking but gazing. Not asking but feeling, being, aching, brimming.

We retraced our safe steps, followed our tracks, crossed the boundary of heaven to earth, scrambled down the ridge of twisted trees, and stumbled at dusk into camp for a welcoming bowl of Bernard's minestrone and blackened biscuits on a stick.

I have thought often of that venture. Had the crevasse opened, we would both be gone—one in a sudden slide and shout, and the other, me, after a brief hesitation before the rope jerked taut.

I see us there, two specks against the splendid glare of white, hopeful, breathless, joined in life or doom as one. My brother, though gone, still leads me across that steep.

## ORDEAL

Though in private our childhood bond was evolving, in public my brother and I seemed to be the dynamic duo. We were co-moderators of the Presbyterian Youth at church. And we were the first double Senior Patrol Leaders in our scout troop. We got along in almost every way, agreed on most things, and could work well together. In church, Bret was in charge of the discussions, and it was my job to ask questions if no one else said anything—to get things going. Some meetings consisted of a conversation between my brother and me, while the other kids nodded. Not always, but once in a while.

In Scouts, Bret did the planning and ran the meetings, and I was quartermaster—in charge of the troop store of miscellaneous camping gear, which I packed into the closet at the Congregational Church where we had our meetings.

One night an Eagle Scout representing Skyloo Lodge of the Order of the Arrow came to the troop meeting and managed an election to select candidates for the ordeal, and potential membership in the lodge. The question he posed: "If you were lost in the woods, what one member of your troop would you like to have with you for safety and good leadership?"

There was no need to think that through: I voted for my brother. But he voted for me. And by some alchemy in the troop's mood that night, the two of us tied. So they sent us both to the coast for the initiatory ordeal.

We arrived after dark on a Friday night in late September. There were maybe thirty boys representing as many troops. We were not to eat that night, or to speak. With our packs on our backs, we followed a member of the order, tall and stern, single file through hills of sand. He carried a torch that crackled, sticky with pitch, and we stumbled along behind him. Now and then he gestured with the torch to a place on the ground, and the next scout in line would drop his pack and begin to lay out his bed for the night as the line, and the light, moved away.

My brother was directed to a dark swale and I, next in line, to a low saddle just beyond. I burrowed in, my snaky body shaping the sand to hold me, and slept easy under the stars.

As dawn came, I needed a walking stick. It seemed I always needed a walking stick. Actually, I needed something to whittle. So I found a hazel wand in a thicket, cut it to shoulder-high length, and began with swift cross-strokes to trim the end. The knife, newly sharpened for the occasion, nicked the knuckle of my left index finger. Before blood came, I could see white deep in the notch. By Boy Scout training, I sat down to diminish the danger of shock, wrapped my knuckle in my official kerchief, and raised my hand high to slow the bleeding. I was light-headed for a few moments but okay.

As instructed, I had gathered my bundle, and when the rangy guide returned, leading other recovered sleepers in single file, I fell in behind the last. When we swung down the hill to pick up my brother, he fell in behind me. We trudged along in silence, until I found a chance to turn to him, and hold up my kerchief-swaddled hand.

"To the bone," I whispered.

His eyebrows went down in reprimand, and he held his finger to his lips, reminding me about our vow of silence.

That day, the older boys, the ones who had survived previous iterations of the ordeal, dropped hints about the fearsome event to come that night. There were oblique references to "most boys . . ." and "with some exceptions . . ." and "rare casualties." I could recognize hype when I heard it, but I saw some faces go pale.

We labored all day to put the camp to bed for the winter—ferrying canoes on our shoulders from the lake to the boathouse, scrubbing the kitchen floor, raking fallen branches from the sand. After an evening meal in silence, we fell into single file again for the journey to the site of our ordeal. We followed our torchbearer for the better part of an hour, twisting back on our tracks at several points, to make the short journey long. And then there was the fire ahead through the trees, with the older boys in Indian getup, feathers, and painted faces.

We stood in a ring around the fire.

"What you are about to witness, you must never tell outside the Order of the Arrow," said the tallest of the older boys. "Do you swear—do not speak! But raise your hand in assent." We raised our hands.

"Your first words will be to accede to the vow you are about to take. First the ordeal, then the vow!"

There is yet in me enough boy to honor that vow. You will get no close detail from me. But in the firelight, fantastic gestures, ritual marking, boys falling to the sand in a swoon. Beside me, my brother stood the test, and so did I. We went forth from there wearing the little bronze arrow on a ribbon hung from a shirt button. We were members of the Order.

Scouting was our calling, until the scoutmaster, feeling brave one night just after marching drill, asked the boys, in a rare spirit of inquiry, "If there was one thing you could change about scouting, what might that be?"

"I would make it all less militaristic," my brother said, speaking first.

"How do you mean?" the scoutmaster asked, after a pause.

"All this marching," my brother said, "this saluting, these ranks, the army green—it's foreign to what we are really about in this world."

"And what is that?"

"Peace," my brother said. The boys shifted where they stood, then returned to attention in their ordered rows.

"Son," the Scoutmaster said, "we all have to serve in the military, eventually. Look what's building up in Vietnam. That's an honor, to serve. We're just here to practice, so we'll be ready for that."

"That's not why I'm here," my brother said. "If that's why others are here, then I must be in the wrong place."

"I'm sorry you feel that way, Bret," the scoutmaster said. "I think, in time, you may understand what I'm saying."

From there the scoutmaster tried to keep the discussion going, but it was a tough go, and soon the meeting ended.

That night, talking in our beds, my brother and I decided our time as scouts had run its course. "We learned a lot," my brother said, "but somehow I think there are other things to do, from here on out."

Recently I found my membership cards from the Order. I see that in 1963 I was an "ordeal" member, but by 1965 I had advanced to a "brotherhood" member. That must have been about the time we stepped away from Skyloo Lodge and from the Scouts.

But some things don't change. If I were lost in the wilderness or marooned in the strange customs of the human world, what one boy would I most want beside me?

No contest.

## SUPER DUPER

TV came to our family late. There were years when we came sniffing around our friends' houses on Saturday mornings, hoping they might invite us in to watch cartoons.

I remember Pat, my best friend across the street, telling me one day that he didn't want to watch TV. "But let's just see what's on," I said. We were addicted to what we did not have.

We heard a report that one neighbor kid told her mother, "At the Staffords, they don't have to just watch TV. They get to go camping and make stuff with tools."

We saw things otherwise. TV was our gold standard for weekend indulgence. And after some years of attrition on their restraint, and the general campaign of the times, our folks finally got a set and placed it in the attic over the garage—a cold and distant place appropriate for this enemy to books. Somehow they got an old couch up there. The spiders arrived on their own. You lowered the ladder, took a flashlight, and headed up into the low-clearance darkness for a bout of sweet pop culture.

Eventually the TV migrated to the living room, and our prime watching years began. Stories from those shows—*My Three Sons, Bonanza, The Life of Riley*—have receded from my mind, but what I remember was our custom at the commercial break: the sixty-second creation of an ice cream extravaganza we called the Super Duper. For the first few breaks, we scouted the kitchen to see what was on hand—ice cream, bananas, sugar sprinkles, red hots, maraschino cherries, chocolate sauce set to heat on low. It generally took several breaks to get everything lined up on the counter. Then the time came for the two of us to break into a clockwork blur. With the first "Brought to you by . . ." we rocketed to the kitchen and began to customize our bowls with layer upon layer of sweet goo. The goal was to be sitting in front of the set with a complete artistic monster before the show returned.

By my brother's senior year, we had it down.

## REVEREND JIM

According to the parchment form that crackles when I hold it, I made my "Confession of Faith" in November of 1965. I was in the choir; I was a member, and later a co-leader, with my brother, of the Presbyterian Youth; and I tried to break into the church by night to play my clarinet for God. We Youth went on field trips, spilling out of a bus in the Oregon desert to view a rainbow by the full moon. We read our Good Book, where I first found the startling Song of Songs. We replaced the deacons and took collection one Sunday each year, passing the brass bowls with green felt lining row by row. We did fund drives for causes I forget. We painted a storefront in the poor section of our city. And we lived in dark wild mystery about the facts of passion, anger, honesty, and love.

The main minister in our church was a much respected man. He knew his Bible. He attended to his duties with a professionalism that mirrored the successful lives of his flock. Then came an offer of a higher salary at a larger church somewhere in California, and he left. I remember his last sermon. Of perhaps hundreds I heard from him, I remember this:

> Every night before I go to sleep, I turn to my wife and say, "I love you." I have done this every night for the eighteen years of our marriage. Often, I know this is an empty phrase, a habit, a few common words. But I say them when they are empty to keep them there. I say them every night because they can be true. And when I realize I do love my wife, the words are there. . . . Let us pray.

Then he was gone down the denominational highway of Presbyterianism, and for a year his associate pastor, Reverend Jim, filled in while a committee of elders searched for the new minister. We all knew Jim was an applicant, and we watched him preach each sermon as part of an episodic job interview, citing text and topic to work the round of the church year.

Then one Sunday, in the folded sheet of pastel paper, the weekly bulletin a pastel hostess handed out as we entered the sanctuary, we saw that a new pastor had been chosen, and it was not Jim. Jim rose to give his last sermon. His crew cut bristled and his face shone with excitement.

"Dearly beloved," he said, "this past year I have watched you all as you prayed and sang, as you listened to my meditations on what we call the issues of the religious life. I have watched the parking lot fill with your long cars and heard the clank of change hit the collection plate. I have talked to you about the Bible, and the news, the safe news, the distant news. But today I want to talk about something deeper, or maybe I should say shallower, than the official version. I want to talk about hypocrisy—your hypocrisy, and mine."

There is a sound in a congregation when people wake up, a sound like wind riffling the pages of a Bible left outside. Like a flame that whispers everywhere at once.

"I want to talk about Vietnam," said Pastor Jim, "and about money, and about the cruelty of lies, and about the sins of comfort. When my sermon today is done, you may not want to ever see me again. You may not agree with me, and you may not agree with each other, but you will remember this day, this Sunday, I promise you."

I remember everyone sitting straight, perfectly still. Even I, my brother, my sisters, sat straight and still. Our father, who often dozed in church, was awake for this one. For the sermon was a species of joyful fire, a flame that hungered and fed. And when the collection plates had been gathered in by the deacons in a trance, and the choir sang the Doxology for Jim's last time, we all filed out to the narthex in silence.

That sermon has never been equaled, in my experience. But the deeper thing, the part that stays with me at my core, happened that evening, at the meeting of the Presbyterian Youth, when Pastor Jim gave his last talk to my brother and me, and to our friends.

We were gathered in the upstairs Sunday School room, and the cookies had turned to crumbs on our laps. Pastor Jim had us in a circle of tan folding chairs. He sat quietly, looking around as we brushed our hands together to shake away the crumbs and fiddled with our empty punch cups, waiting. I was fifteen. Something about his manner had silenced us.

Then he stood, crossed the room, and closed the door. Once he was settled in his chair again, he looked around the room and smiled.

"I need to tell you something," he said, "that I suspect no one has told you. It's a subject parents may find difficult, but it must be said. Please forgive me if you find this subject awkward. I do, too, but I must go on."

We looked at each other, and then at the floor or out the window. I looked at him: crew cut, pale blue knit shirt, black-framed glasses. He took a deep breath.

"You must be absolutely alone," he said, "and you must know you will not be interrupted—when you first make love to someone." He paused. His stare was level. He looked at me, at Carolyn, at my brother, Marilyn, Paul, Chuck, Nicolette, all around the circle. He gave everyone his look. "There is only one first time, and no matter where you go from this experience, or who you may be with, after, this time will always be sacred."

In my mind the Bible was on fire, the Song of Solomon was being sung aloud, my dreams were being spoken by this plain-looking man with a clear voice.

"Sacred," he said. "I do not use this word lightly. Sacred. Pay attention with all you have in this time together, as close as you have ever been with another person. Feel what you feel. Be kind to one another. This is one of life's greatest gifts, God knows. So do not hurry."

It seemed there was no oxygen in the room. We lived on some other form of elixir.

"And after, do not brag. This private time will be with you all your life. Feel what you feel. Guard what you learn. Learn to love."

"You must be in a space where there is no hurry," he said again. "I need to tell you this very clearly, because there is so much in our culture that gives you a different idea: You must know that no one will interrupt you, because you are about to enter into a time that is yours alone, you two, and you need to be there slowly, and know exactly what you feel. This is not a place for your parents, or for your friends. This is only for the two of you. Love can happen, and be beautiful, and not leave scars on your heart, if you make it your own, in private, without fear, without ambition or pride. Take care of this other person you lie down with. Sensation is a treasure. It is not designed for the backseat of a car, or a room in the house at a party where others might surprise you. Find a beautiful place and make it holy together. I am talking about love, and spirit, and a kind of light that settles over all the world when you come to this gently."

There was no sound in the room. We were a tableaux of figures. My brother with his lips slightly parted, staring far away. The twins, Carolyn and Marilyn askew, and Paul, the saxophone player from the high school band.

"You may not find the person this first time, the partner you will be with always. But you must find honesty. The first person you are with will always be part of who you are, will shape your loving ever after. Be private, be honest, and feel what you feel."

Then Reverend Jim leaned back, as if shaking off a set of chains.

"I have enjoyed my time with you," he said. "But before I left this church, I felt I needed to say these things to you. I wish you well."

It had rained when we came out of the church, and the parking lot was dark. Some parents came to fetch us home. I looked back at the open door where Pastor Jim stood, watching us go. He wasn't the Reverend any more. Just a figure in the dark doorway.

"We need to hurry," said the driver of my car, someone's father, "get you kids home for dinner." I put my fingers to the textured trim by the window as we drove away.

I don't remember talking with my brother about this amazing feat of telling. It was as if a code kept us in our separate cells of silence. Where does such a sermon, said slowly and in private, reside in a young person's life?

When I hopped a freight at midnight later that spring, to serenade Carolyn with my clarinet, and was chased from her house by the family dog, I thought of Reverend Jim. When our father, before I left for college, told me nothing in detail about sex, or women, or each lonely man as a seeker after solace, I thought of Reverend Jim. When I kissed a girl for the first time in the winter of 1968, I thought of Reverend Jim. And as that girl and I, my wife and I entered intimacy on our wedding night, dwelt there for some years, then drifted away from intimacy over a decade of slow departure, I thought of Reverend Jim.

The first time. Sacred. The Bible on fire. Feel what you feel . . . guard what you learn . . . learn to love.

Who schooled me in truth telling? Was it my father, the great poet? Was it my teachers in school? Was it the great books that guided me into teaching? Well, in some ways, yes. But at heart I am still in the presence, in the care, under the guidance of that stalwart teller of difficult things, Reverend Jim.

## DARKNESS

For some reason, I felt safe in the dark. Night was my friend. It was not a place of danger but a place where you could hide from danger. And if there was a moon, you could have it all: deep shadows and a path of light.

Inner darkness, on the other hand, was not so easy. My brother seemed assured in school, threw himself into class projects and social events. He explained dating to me, encouraged me to give it a try, but I demurred. When I spoke in class, my face turned crimson. It was just so hard to be a human. I could be a raccoon, skulking around in the trees. I could climb an old maple and wait for dawn. I could sleep on a hillside alone. But to speak, to rely on response to certain poor performance—that was darkness.

Years later I visited my old high school to talk with an English class. While waiting for the bell, my cue, I sat in the library where I had spent

many hours, days, years as a student. Three boys came in, maybe sopho-
mores by their look. They sat down at a table with four chairs, and one of
them put his foot up on the seat of the empty chair. They were talking,
ducking their heads, looking around. Then a lone boy entered the library.
It was clear they knew him; their heads bobbed slightly. As he approached
the table, he looked at the empty chair. In that moment I remembered the
whole code: that glance meant "Can I sit there? Am I welcome? Do you see
me? Am I a person? Do I exist . . . ?"

The boy with his foot on the chair did not move. And he did not look up.
The lone boy paused almost imperceptibly, then chose a table with no one,
out in the middle of the whispering library where, I now saw, several packs
of young creatures, alert to danger and alive to the shifting alliances of their
tribe, guarded their territory.

Then I remembered suicide. In high school I thought about suicide.
Every other remedy required so many steps, most of which I could not do
well. Learn to talk to people? Get invited to things? Do things with people I
didn't know? Graduate? Have a girl? Get married? My God!

"Hey," a kid shouted in my direction in the hall one morning. "Why don't
you come over after school?"

Helplessly, my face brightened. Then I heard a voice behind me.

"Sounds great! Shall we take the boat out?"

"If we feel like it."

When I look at such a moment now, I have to delve deep to find what
was at stake. So a rich person shows off the prerogatives of wealth, of favor
bestowed or denied. So what? Well, when you are in the long, tender passage
from the chrysalis of childhood, a few syllables in such an encounter can
cut like knives.

Some days, all I could do was put one foot in front of the other. On the
bus, a guy named Ben shouted to a guy named Jerry, "Hey, that Andrea—
did you put it in her?" "Why the hell not?" The shouts were so mean—to
Andrea, to everyone, to me. What about love? What about tenderness? Did I
fit in this world? Maybe I should just . . .

I remember clearly the moment when the suicide option left me. I was sitting in the back row in Senior English class. Mrs. Pittman was about to hand back our papers on the Chaucer unit, and I realized I wasn't that interested in what I got on my paper. I was interested in what would happen—not just today, but tomorrow, the next year, when I moved away, when I got old. I was curious about the world. Nuclear annihilation? That seemed fairly likely in those days. But I—this is perverse—I wanted to be there. I wanted to see it. I wanted to know how people would behave—I, and others. And pollution—would the rivers die? Would people change? Would people do good in the world? Was it just one long ride to doom? What kind of doom? What would happen?

I was just so curious. I realized as Mrs. Pittman came down my row, that I was too damn curious to cut it short.

## "DID THE WORLD THANK UNCLE BRET?"

There is no question: my brother was a saint. He showed this in many ways. But as a high school junior, he reached his pinnacle. At our school, there was some kind of manufactured inter-class rivalry that positioned American capitalism at the heart of fevered teenage zest. Each class competed against the others in a calendar of drives—the sophomore class used-battery drive . . . the junior class cookie drive . . . the senior class old car bash. For a dollar, you could take a swing with a sledge hammer at the doors of an old Desoto on blocks in the senior parking lot—or five dollars for a swing at a window.

But when my brother volunteered to be the Junior Class Extra Projects Committee Chairman—a decidedly lesser role for anyone but him—he went the distance. He dug deep into his aspirations and worked long hours to make a miracle happen. Before anyone really knew what was coming, he had the local nursery donate a hundred flowering cherry trees, the Country Club give permission to plant them in a mile-long row north of the golf course, and three hundred students promise to bring shovels and gloves and squander a beautiful spring Saturday to make the world a better place.

A lowly sophomore, I took my bike to watch the spectacle. All those kids digging holes, mixing mysterious powders the nursery had provided, unwrapping burlap from the root balls of all those delicate saplings and tamping them gently into place, hauling water in buckets from neighbors along the road. Traffic stopped by the local cops, cars honking and people waving. And in the middle of it all, seemingly everywhere at once, my big brother, the magician of the beautiful, the leader of the young.

I remember how compact he was. He had begun, mysteriously, to not be as tall as me. But that day, light came from inside him. A deep delight.

Years later, after he was gone, I was driving with my daughter Rosie along Country Club Road on a Saturday morning in April. She was eight, and Bret's trees were on fire with blossoms, spilling soft light where they billowed in their long, winding line.

"Dad," Rosie said, "did the world ever thank Uncle Bret for those trees?"

"No," I said. "I don't think the world really did."

That night, after I had dropped Rosie at her mother's house, I lay in the back room of my rental on Custer and thought about that day in 1965 when my brother was fully the man he had become. Out my window, the big cherry tree in my yard flickered softly in the dark.

"Thank you, my brother."

## OUR ROAD

There is a road near where I live that winds through forest. Improbable in the city, such a dark place on a night drive in town. That forest was wild when I was a child—it was what we called the Woods when we played there, wandering in freedom close to home. It has become Tryon Creek State Park, and the road we called Terwilliger Extension is now simply southwest Terwilliger Boulevard.

But the dark stretch of road remains. When I drive our mother along that road at night, without fail, when we leave the last house light behind and start along the mile that is yet dark, she will say, "Now it's our road."

Our road. Now it doesn't belong to anyone but us.

Did she say this to our father, when he was alive—whenever they came to a dark stretch of highway and were gliding along together? Did she say this to her father, or her father to her, when they found a dark stretch of road? Is this what she has always said to herself, with anyone, once the lit landmarks of the human fall behind, and she is embarked on a journey without signs?

I travel such a road myself. The passage through these stories of my brother runs dark. I don't believe it is "our road." It is my road, mine with my brother, my memory of my brother. The stories I remember, the glimmers here and there along the dark trace—who else remembers what I do, or as I do? I'm sure I have some things wrong. But this is a dark road, and I need to account for dark things, half-forgotten things, even things created out of need in order to name what I cannot understand.

"This is our road," our mother says again, as the dim silhouettes of trees along Terwilliger flash by. And I realize, silent at the wheel, that it takes many roads to make our road. Each must tell how things came to be by their own lights, their own long nights.

## "YOU SAID YOU WOULD BE HOME"

Our father the poet could be very close and kind, and he could also be a distant enigma. As a friend wrote to me after William Stafford died, "Your father's lively elusiveness or what might feel like remoteness is honestly and decently connected to his art, to his spirit, to his ethics. . . . [This remoteness] is the key to his capacity for beginnings, for near-epiphanies, near-escapes from despair. Yet of course it would come with a price. For him, for those who loved him."

At home, our father was a gentle person, in many ways. A good listener, generous with help. As a writer, he believed in following quiet signals in the language in search of "what was there," rather than imposing some prior intention on his fluid, intuitive process.

As a parent, he was tolerant, to a point. For days things would flow along in the genial cooperative music of our family ways.

But now and then, there was law. I think my brother felt this more than I. The older, the one whose middle name, William, was our father's name, Bret was accountable in a way I was not. He was number-one son.

In one early iteration of this, as recorded in our father's journal when Bret was nine, the outcome was, finally, conciliatory: "Tonight Bret stayed out till ten. We waited up for him and looked silently when he came in— the purpose was to make him feel, not triumphant at breaking a rule, but worry at violating an understanding. Not sure we did right, tho we ended with friendliness."

Despite the happy ending to this account, I am arrested by the understory. Rules are replaced by understandings, and understandings are enforced by silence, and the whole arrangement is carried out by plan.

The first time my brother went on a date in high school, it was cause for celebration. "Take the car. Need some money? Have a good time."

But behind the generous spirit of the occasion, there was a law: a certain time for Bret's return. Was it 9 p.m.? 10? I don't know. What I do know is that Bret was late. And when he returned, the house was locked. He knocked. No answer. He waited, colder. He was made "to think about it."

I don't remember any of this. The occasion somehow passed me by. Was I away? Asleep? I don't know. I only know this story from our mother's telling. For her, it was a story about Bill, the quixotic poet, unpredictable, "friendly but not tame." Now and then, she tells the story as part of the mystery of him.

I hear the story as an episode in the formation of Bret. I see him standing on the porch, the glow of his first date ebbing away. The family car ticking in the driveway. Alone at home, in the strange, dark puzzle of Number-One Son.

# BOOK III. HAVE SWEET DREAMS

# A CORNFIELD IN IOWA

When my brother left the family to go to college, he reenacted the long-standing migrational passage of the Stafford clan: he went to the Midwest heartland. Not the Kansas of our father, or the Nebraska of our mother, but to Iowa, where we had lived when he was three. He enrolled at Grinnell, a small college in a small town on the endless prairie.

When he returned at Christmastime, the first evening he rolled out his sleeping bag in the living room rather than sleep in the room we had shared in high school. Maybe his bed was gone by then. I can't remember. I had made our room my own in some way. He did not feel it was his anymore.

We asked him about college, expecting a big report. But he didn't say much. It was going okay. He had some good classes. He'd been on some hikes.

"It's a little town, like we used to live in. Like North Manchester." (His first-grade year, when we lived in North Manchester, Indiana, still had a hold on his mind.)

But as to details of really engaging professors, or social life, girls, activities, he didn't have much to say. And later that spring, he suggested to me that we enroll together at the University of Oregon in Eugene.

"What about Grinnell?"

"I'm ready to come back to Oregon."

His grades from Grinnell had been mailed to the folks: C average. That was not my brother's style. Something had changed.

Years later, after our time in college together, and after his own orbiting journey almost to escape velocity into Canada, when he was struggling to get back to Oregon, as I have said earlier, he did not want the word "Grinnell" on his résumé. I never understood why, not until long after, when I had a chance to go there.

I was with a group of writers, barnstorming the country to engage college students and their communities with nearby nature. We would come to a town, invite the students to take us for a tramp in some natural space they knew—coast, forest, prairie—and then we would hold a series of writing workshops and readings to celebrate connections between the human community and the natural world.

When we came to Grinnell, my mind was on high alert. What was this place, and what had it done to my brother?

A group took us to a prairie restoration project that several generations of students had helped to create. Ten years ago, we were told, there was one species of life on this three-hundred acre plot: corn. Now the corn was gone, and the species count was over 350: big bluestem grass, wild turkeys, burr oak. . . . They took us with pride and delight from one life to the next.

"This was barren," the oldest professor said, spreading his arms to take in the little Eden he had helped to restore, "and now look."

The oldest professor. He was my source. When I had a chance, as the students and the other writers rambled over the rolling hills, I took him aside.

"My brother was here," I said, "for one year—the fall of 1966 to the spring of 1967. Were you here then? Can you tell me what it was like?"

He looked at me, and then looked far over the beautiful land. "That was the last of the worst," he said. "The last year of hell."

I felt a chill crawl up my back.

"The level of hazing for first-year students," he said, "was catastrophic. I was just starting my teaching, and I didn't know what to expect. On one occasion, I went to visit one of my students in his residence hall. There was filth of all kinds—and I don't just mean dirt. It was unspeakable. Some of the things the students did to each other—take them out in a cornfield, and—" He paused. "I wouldn't have believed it if I didn't hear verbatim."

"What did you hear?"

"It finally got so bad," he said, "that students were getting injured, but the psychological hurt was surely deeper and harder to see. We could hardly do college with some of those young men after the upperclassmen had their way. Finally, the president got wind of it. Strange how sometimes the leader is the last to know. Anyway, he summoned one of the ringleaders, an upperclassman who got caught, to his office. I was there with several other faculty. The president started grilling this young man about the hazing rituals. At first, the student was reticent. But once he got going, you could tell he relished what he was describing: students stripped naked in the snow, made to endure taunts and challenges, made to feel helpless, until they swore loyalty and service to their betters.

"At a certain stage of this testimony—it had turned into some kind of perverse bragging—at a certain stage, the student fell silent for a moment, and from across the room I could hear the president's teeth grinding together. He was so furious, it brought out an animal response in him. I'm a biologist, so I notice such things. He was like the alpha lion, and this jackal was threatening his young."

"The next year, fall of '67, it all changed. One thing changed it all. You see, they had all the men's dormitories in a cluster. That built a kind of pack dynamic that let the boys run their own cruel show. But fall, 1967, they shook it up, alternated the dorms boy-girl-boy-girl. Women's dorm, then men's, then women's. And later they alternated floors within the dorms. And you know what? The girls tamed the boys, civilized them. We had other kinds of problems after that, had to increase the sex ed and all. But the cruelty stopped cold."

We both looked at the prairie, the students leading each other to various episodes of color, pattern, and life.

"Scores went up, too," the professor said. "Students had a chance to be in college after that." The wind had picked up, and the grass seemed to flow toward the horizon.

Early the next morning I walked through the silent campus and down into the town. Sleeping houses, old trees, the long sky reaching like religion over all the humans had made of the open land. On Fifth, I came to the post office, and peered through glass at the recruiting poster—a soldier with an infrared eyepiece and a small cannon in his arms. Across the street was a chapel and a statue of the Virgin with her bare foot crushing a serpent.

I thought of my brother here, trying to negotiate manliness, tenderness, sex and sin while under brutal assault by soldiers of the upper class.

In the one letter my brother sent home from Grinnell, in the midst of reports of a dance, a conversation at the Christian group, and a friend planning to go to Mexico over spring break, he makes one oblique reference to the hidden world of initiatory hell: "We go to the Amana Colonies," he writes, "an old German colony, where I hear we will be served the best food in Iowa. Each of us 'preps' are to put on an imitation of an upperclassman. I am hoping that no enemies will be made."

After our visit to Grinnell, the writers traveled to the Amana Colony near Iowa City. We sat in the chapel there, a room sparely furnished with pine pews, while an elder woman of the community, Harriet, told us of the customs of this old sect, called among themselves "The Community of True Inspiration."

"I remember," Harriet said at one point, "the years of the loud amen." She told of an era of fervent belief, of beautiful community, happy young people, old ways sustaining the good life.

As she spoke, I sat on a pine bench near the back of the sanctuary and thought of my brother. I remembered his years of loud amen—the times when he was powerful in who he could be, a beautiful, gentle, wise young man. ·

We got up to say goodbye to Harriet, and I felt sudden tears as I took her hand. I couldn't explain why, but she looked at me with understanding.

"You are a true child of Amana," she said.

When I returned to Oregon, I told our mother about my strong feeling at Amana.

"Of course you felt that," she said. "When we lived in Iowa City and you boys were little, we used to take you out to Amana. Such a sweet little village. It was always so peaceful there."

"Iowa," she said. "Amana. Maybe that's why Bret went to Grinnell."

Long after my brother's passing, his letters from Grinnell have surfaced in the family attic. From September 11, 1966, there is an account of one episode of hazing:

> The upperclassmen in Clark Hall have fun initiating the freshmen. A few nights ago, at one o'clock, they blindfolded all of us, led us stumbling in the dark through the town and out into the country. After about an hour, they took our blindfolds off and asked us to get some stack corn, then left us. By knowing which direction we had been going, and checking the position of the moon and north star on that quiet night, we were able, with pillowcases full of corn, to find our way back to town and the college. Here, we spelled out "Clark" in twenty-foot letters of corn on the main field. I believe the initiations are now over with.

But I believe there were other, more brutal episodes he did not speak of. His letters from that year often substitute statements of loyalty to the family for any account of struggle: "Surely there is much more for me to say, but I am afraid I cannot think of it now. Anyway, the most important thing is that everyone should be happy. I hope you all are."

## THE WATER TOWER

When I was very young, as I have said, my favorite toy was night. It was big, and it was mine. When the house door opened on darkness, a room that no one knew had become my own.

Trees were second place among my toys back then—how they held out their arms to be climbed. Water may have been a close third, the way it surrenders but does not obey, schooling my soul in pliable independence. But night was the great implement for endless venturing. There was a kind of hidden music everywhere in darkness, humming below what the ears could hear.

My brother played the violin, and I the clarinet. Our sisters played recorder, and piano. Now when I try to imagine the sound of my practicing, I don't know why they didn't all go insane. I could summon quite an aria of squeaks and squawks. And my brother's violin, early on, competed with my terrors. But gradually, the sounds we made began to resemble music. Bret put his violin aside sometime in junior high, except for carols at Christmas, but I kept at the clarinet, and worked up in particular the adagio from Mozart's Concerto in A. Quiet, ethereal, of the night—that song was my theme.

When I was little, it is reported, I once told our mother at evening, "I'm going out to get the nice feel of the night." Night was soft, I remember, and safe. Where others might feel fear in the dark, I felt refuge. How did I get to be that way? I don't know. But I was always a night wanderer. If you listened in the dark you could hear your heart. You could ignore the boundaries of daylight—fence, safety, propriety. You could know what it will be like after dying—to be a spirit, nameless, harmless, affectionate, curious, and free.

Some of my early ventures happened in junior high, when I announced one evening that I wanted "to see dawn from the dark side," and would be gone when others woke.

"Tell us what you find out," our father said. So I set an alarm, and when it went off, I apologized to my brother, told him to sleep. Soon, his breathing changed, and I could go. I slipped out of the house at about 4 a.m., walked our town's dark streets to the place we called "the abandoned farm," maybe a mile west, threaded my way by starlight on a known path past the burned house, the fallen shed, to an old maple tree I had climbed often. By memory, my hands found the handholds, and I hoisted myself to a perch on a fat horizontal limb. There I sat waiting, listening, watching, thinking. This was my true home. Dawn came slowly, a change in the feel of the air, then the look of the light at the far horizon. Then a murmuring of birds, and a shift in dewfall, and then, after long overture, the sun.

I remember wishing it could be dark again. There was so much more to see in the velvet splendors.

The year my brother went off to college, all need for explanation vanished. I simply went forth as I pleased, once our house was quiet with sleep. Then in the dark I would cross the street to the water tower, painted dun green, surrounded by old fir trees with their tops cut off at about sixty feet, the height of the tower. There was a ladder we had often fumbled at as kids. The bottom dozen rungs were covered by a hinged steel plate locked shut We had seen workers swing the plate away, and climb the ladder to the top. But when they left, they always locked the plate again, and we could not climb.

But now I was sixteen, and such paltry obstructions were not to be borne. By dark, I found a way to hoist myself above the plate, and climb at will. The first time, a chill gripped me as I willed myself higher. "Maybe I will die" were the words that went through my mind. I had to accept that. "This is so cool."

At the top, the tower had a dome. You crawled up the slope to where the very top was flat, and you could lie down, and look up. Did I mention the moon was full? Did I mention it was a rare warm night in late September? Now that I had crossed over the boundary from obedience to whim, I took off my clothes, and lay in the moonlight, savoring the nectar of my freedom.

As the weeks went on, my forays went farther. If you followed Iron Mountain Boulevard past our old grade school, you came to Country Club Road, where my brother had planted the hundred trees. And beyond that road, if you climbed the fence, you could cross the golf course, leaving tracks in the dewy grass under the moon. And beyond that, you could follow a steep little road down to the railroad track. And if you followed the rail line west for a couple miles, you could walk up a path tunneling through dark trees to the church—our church, the Lake Grove Presbyterian Church.

And at the church, there was a wisteria vine that climbed to the flat roof over the Fellowship Hall. And if you crossed that roof, you came to the skylight. And if you could get that open, you could drop through and be inside. At least that's how it all worked in my mind one day during seventh-period senior history class. Mr. Satchell was talking about the Civil War, and I was walking the tracks in my mind.

It took me several nights to get this far, every night a bit farther, but once I was on the roof, I had a plan: Next time I would bring my clarinet, and inside the tall dark of the sanctuary, I could play a serenade for God. I imagined Mozart's yearning, and mine, climbing like a thread of incense toward heaven.

Trouble was, I couldn't get the skylight open. Even after trying all the blades on my boy scout knife, I couldn't get it.

Hence Plan B. For the first time in some time, the next Sunday I said I would stay for Sunday School. "I can walk home. It's easy."

"Easy?" our father said.

"Well, yeah." So I was at Sunday School, saw some old friends, the saints who still attended, and then I dawdled around, reading a hymnal or something, until everyone was gone. Then I opened the latch on every window on the second story, and took my leave.

That night, I took my clarinet, slipped out of the house, crossed the golf course, followed the railroad track (cradling my clarinet in my arms so it would be warm, and tuneful, once I was inside), tunneled up the path under dark trees, climbed the wisteria vine at the church wall, padded across the flat roof to those windows, and tried them one by one. All locked. Damn! Back down the vine, along the track, over the rolling hills, up the road to our house, and into bed.

The next Sunday, I followed the same routine: unlocking all the windows. And that night, the same result: windows locked. What an unfortunate coincidence, I thought. Halfway back along the tracks, I had to lie down a few feet from the rail to sleep. The train whistle shrilled me awake, and I plunged down the embankment in the dark to wait for it to pass so I could get on home.

Again, on the following Sunday morning, I came out of my room at 8:30, dressed for church.

"You didn't used to like Church," my sisters said to me.

"Yeah, well, things change."

"Maybe there's a gir-rul?"

"Don't be ridiculous."

So the folks had to go to church, and after the service, over cookies in the Fellowship Hall, I told them they could go, and I would walk home after Sunday School.

"What about your good shoes?"

"I'll be careful."

So they went their way, and I climbed the stairs to Sunday School, greeting the saints, dawdling, then, when all were gone, to the windows. This time there was a note wedged into the window frame. The words were written with intensity: "Whoever you are, DO NOT mess with these latches."

The janitor was on to me. So my plan, Mozart for God, was foiled.

But I was not to be deterred. What was it? There was this pressure in my body that could not be otherwise released. It had to pour forth as music in darkness, or I would suffocate. So the next night, I followed my accustomed route, but then went farther along the track, beyond the path to church, until I came to a siding where a freight train idled. I came up on the dark side, and climbed onto the ladder at the rear of one of the cars. Soon, the train started slowly moving west. I decided I would ride until the pace was almost too fast for me to jump, and then I would jump.

What I did not know was the primary rule for riding unseen: When the train turns, if you are on the outside, the convex side of the train, no one can see you. But when the train turns the other way, if you lean too far out on the concave side, you stand revealed.

The tracks turned, I leaned out, there was a shout, a whistle, and the train started slowing down. I jumped off, and thrashed my way down into a blackberry thicket, burrowed into darkness. Someone came with a light, swiveled the beam over my thicket, then pitched a few stones, hoping to get lucky. In time, the light disappeared, and the train began to move. When it was gone, I climbed out of my thicket, wiped blood from my scratches, and soldiered on. After a bit, I turned off onto a quiet road, and this brought me to the house of the Hale twins—Carolyn and Marilyn. If I could not send my musical soul to God, they would have to do.

Did I mention the moon was full? It was. I took the clarinet in pieces from the case lined in velvet, and fit the pieces together, warming the ebony and silver against my chest, then fit the reed to the mouthpiece, blew a few breaths quietly through the instrument to warm the wood, and began to play.

The aria begins low, and climbs a few tentative steps. Then low again, it climbs again. This was my soul's path, and I spoke it with all I had.

I was just getting to the part where the soul gets to speak from on high, when I heard a screen door slam, and Carolyn's voice call out, "Is that the radio?" Then there was a frenzy of barking, the Hale dog charged toward me, and I fled. Grabbing my case on the ground with one hand, and gripping the clarinet with the other, I high-tailed it down that road. By the time the dog turned back, my heart was pounding, and I could feel my sweat biting into the blackberry scratches on my legs and arms.

As I began the long walk home—climbing to the tracks and heading east—the moon began to dim. I looked up. The eclipse. I forgot that was coming. The tracks before me grew darker and darker. I had to stop and wait for it to pass, so I could stumble onward in my deep fatigue.

Later, at school, Carolyn approached me during the ten-minute break.

"Was that you—eclipse night? It sounded like you."

"Yes, it was me."

"Why didn't you come in? We set the alarm to see the eclipse, and when we got up to let the dog out, there was this music. But then Tippy went crazy, and you stopped. It was cool. But you should have come in."

I could tell her I stopped because of the dog. But I couldn't tell her then, or anyone in those days, nor did she ask why it was I was out there in the dark trying to play Mozart under the moon.

Can I say it now, my brother? Maybe I can say it for you: There is something inside a boy, not yet man, that has almost no chance. To show this thing would be taken wrong, surely, cause pain, steel your resolve for utter reticence. This wordless treasure could not come forth as it is felt within. When I looked down naked on our town, when I walked the midnight rails, when I climbed the vine, and finally tried to play my heart, I was apart from the trials to come—sex, money, résumé, family, and all the rest. By some language of pure light, I and the moon could send the best of the boy in safety beyond the man.

## KESTER

A week before spring break of 1967, my brother appeared back in Oregon, and announced that the two of us were going to check out Eugene.

"How'd you get here so soon," I asked. "Did you have to cut class?"

"It doesn't matter," Bret said. "The point is, classes will be in session at the University of Oregon, and that's what we want to see."

I had applied to Stanford—announcing in my application essay that my life goal was to live as Thoreau had lived—but was not accepted. Doubtless some worthy on the admissions committee had remarked that this dreamer could live in a hut somewhere without the inconvenience of a Stanford education. So, yes, Eugene sounded good.

We took the family car and one piece of advice from our father: "Say hello to my old friend Kester Svendsen, on the faculty in English." We said we would.

The two-hour drive south from Portland began in silence. My brother had become a silent person I didn't know. But gradually, the miles rolled by—through Salem, across the Santiam River, and on south across the flat, fertile farmland of the Willamette Valley—and we got back to brotherhood.

"So, Mendelphoze," I said, "how shall we do this?"

"How about that Kester guy, Señor?"

"Oh yeah, let's check the English Department. Like Daddy said."

At the office in PLC, the skyscraper on campus, we were informed that Professor Svendsen was about to teach his advanced Shakespeare class over in Commonwealth Hall. Since we were family friends, maybe it would be okay to sit in. We promised to ask Kester before class started, and strode forth into the spring sunshine to seek Commonwealth Hall. There was a friendly feel to the air. The drive had marked our distance from home—far enough to be free, close enough to take home dirty laundry on the weekends. And there she was, the naked, polished bronze of the Indian maiden holding out a leaf to her fawn—right there in front of the Art Museum. (How many boys like us did she recruit to the university?) This was our place.

Kester's class, it turned out, was dynamite. It was toward the end of his career, and he brought everything to his teaching. I remember his remark to the class that they should read each scene in *Lear* seven times—one for poetry, one for the ideas, one for character, one for an apprehension of how this scene advances the story. . . . And so on. I should have been taking notes! If we happen on a class like this by chance, I thought, this place is very cool.

Of course, it was not by chance. Kester Svendsen was a genius and had cancer, I learned later. He spoke that day with the fierce abandon of a tragic muse. Being there with my brother to witness his passion formed our destiny.

Driving north that evening, based on one academic hour, and the Indian maiden—and, most telling, having my brother back—it was clear we would go to Oregon together. In my room—our room at home, we filled out our applications to the UO Honors College together, even breaking into our old song now and then. We both were accepted. Bret arranged his transfer from Grinnell, and when summer came, we looked forward to taking on the world together come September.

## PURITAN PLEASURES

Bret went on down to Eugene early in September. He had a room in Collier Hall. I would follow. I would have a room in Stafford hall and a roommate, Paul, from high school band. Everything was set. But for my first year away from home, as I blundered into the realm of freedom and love, I was strangely alone from my brother. I was in a tunnel of my own mysteries.

The day before I was to leave home, in late September 1967, I found myself alone with our father. We had just finished our bowls of shredded wheat, and he stood at the counter to pour himself a second round. At the table, I held the old farm bowl with the chipped rim, the one from Nebraska with its blue crow centered when you tilted back your head to drain the last of the milk.

"When I first went away to college," my father began, and by some resonance in his voice I knew exactly what he would do. Now— finally—he would give me the man-to-man talk. Maybe he gave this talk to my brother before me, though Bret had told me nothing. Daddy must have planned this moment for days, planned for a time when the rest of the family would be away, and he could tell me what I needed to know. Now the other good book would open, the one that had stayed sealed until this day, with its proverbs and psalms of pleasure and of creation. The bowl's blue crow trembled in my hands, as he went on.

". . . when I was with women," he said, "I realized they trusted me to decide what was right."

I put the bowl down, and bowed over it. He stood somewhere behind my right shoulder, surely about to go on. I knew so little. I had somehow drifted through the enchanted palace of high school pretty much alone. I had never touched a girl in the way of my vague but insistent dreams. Walking our town's streets at night, I had seen the sky shimmer, felt the young world shake, but touched no one. Now my mind whirled in ignorance. It seems absolutely incredible to me today, but in 1967 I was totally innocent and a fool. What could two bodies do, woman and man together, lips and hands and the rest? My body was virgin, yes, but my mind even more inert. As my father spoke, I could see my passionate ignorance outlined before me, in the air two bright, loving shadows about to be kindled as one as he would describe the configurations of pleasure.

But my father had no more to tell me. I had heard the whole message. Women—and my father—trusted me to decide what was right. We munched our cereal and that was that.

With this thrifty preparation, I left the next morning for Eugene, where thousands of young women and men thronged along streets under bowers of maple. The women shook their long hair, glanced in my direction, and turned slowly away. Sometimes they smiled, and stories came streaming from their eyes. For a moment, I would feel an omnivorous, passionate vertigo, and then they walked on. Among them, I moved like a leaf in the wind, buffeted equally by passion and restraint.

When the maple leaves had fallen, I photographed bare trunks in silhouette on high-contrast film, checked out the Art Department's darkroom key, and stayed up all night to print those shapes for the walls of my room. I remember my favorite image, a tall, metaphoric embrace between two oaks. My ignorance stood boundless, my longing immense.

Strangely, mysteriously, even, in the end, tragically, it was not my custom to ask my brother about such things. Despite our deep connections, there were gaping chasms between us. Maybe we were living a story from Kansas—or more likely Nebraska, the town of Holmesville, that timeless land of my preacher grandfather on our mother's side. If we consider what was going on in 1967, in Eugene, the sexual freedom everyone around me seemed to be displaying (women marching topless down 11th Avenue holding a banner: "Join us—it's legal!"), my spin on things had to be coming from somewhere very distant and very strong. I thought my father's words—"the right thing"—meant you do nothing. Nothing. You are polite, and that means reserved, and that means celibate.

What a bizarre notion.

One month after arriving in Eugene, at the age of seventeen I sat alone in a stairwell in the student union, studying anthropology. The day's reading blurred before me. Rain blurred the tall windows above me, framed in aluminum. Then something in the text brought a tense focus to the light. I read in this big, generic textbook how, among the animals, our human bodies stand and move in unique ways. We do not mate like animals, the book explained; we join together face to face.

Face to face? This was an utter revelation to this puritan boy-child. I remember my eyes slowing their zigzag down the page, and the words jostling to a sudden stop. The book sagged heavy in my hands. I put my pencil in it, and it fell shut. Then I lifted it open and read again: Man and woman face each other when they love.

I sat in a trance. The obvious and the endlessly mysterious had joined, in the loving of woman and man. Some thudding readjustment of memory and imagination shook me.

Can I continue this most amazing display of my ignorance? I must: I had seen dogs mate; I had heard rumors of the lusty couple caught "humping" in the basement of the dorm. All brash haste. These missed what I felt might possibly be true. To my amazement now, a way remained for the kind of tenderness I felt.

This basic information had come late to my mind, but it had a room prepared there, and it took my heart by storm. I had to walk the streets all that night. Death would come, but sleep? Impossible.

My path outward from my impasse began not with love but with landscape. My brother had found a place north from Florence on the Oregon coast where I first came that spring of 1968. He drew me a map on an envelope and sent me there. You park on the shoulder of Highway 101 and step through an opening in the interwoven forest wall of contorted shore pine, spruce, and salal. You follow a trail like a tunnel down toward the boom of the surf, a sandy path worn so deep, the surface of the ground rambles at eye-level, and the salal bush has closed overhead with its small white blooms. You tunnel under wild rhododendron wreathed blossoming in fog, and complete the path down the steep forest dune at a camp hollowed under the tangled canopy of spruce limbs. In those days you had to push through the thicket at the end, to come out into that circle of open ground where people built fire and lay down on the earth. You lived in a kind of den inside the bluff.

I have never met another camper there, but the custom has always been to leave a small stack of firewood under a slab of bark. Often, you find a bundle of kindling, too, split from driftwood cedar, tied with a cord or root. Even in the rain, that dry wood makes one way to be warm.

We have always called that path and its doorway in the trees the "Rabbit Hole." You step into something very old, find your way by foot, smell salt. I went there often alone. Some days, I could do nothing else.

And then things began to change. In my landscape of silence and longing, I met Vera. She stood slender, and had a way of bending close to hear. She stood turned slightly to the side, even more shy than I, so I could talk to her, and then she could talk to me. With her, the idea of talking with a woman felt possible. Talking brought the puritan pleasures I had learned in my half-education at home. All sensation and all pleasures tapered into a path of words. All wish dwindled, compressed along the syllables of the breath. The body held still and apart, while words reached out, a voice in song, a story moving along, a tendril of generosity and sometimes of longing. Love became a silence welling up, or a touching story, but not a physical embrace beyond the family, no touch, never a kiss.

When Vera first met me after class and told me the story of the car in the swimming pool, I fell into this kind of love. I loved the life where strangers meet and tell stories. It seems a car in her hometown released its own brake sometime in the night, and rolled over the curb, down across the lawn, and into the pool of the rich neighbor. Next morning it lay there, deep and cool. They all gathered in the morning, she said, and stared. The car crouched at the bottom of the pool, so clean and still, and they saw an automobile for the first time—helpless, naked, and fair. It could last there forever. It would never wear out, never suffer the touch of rust. They loved what they saw. I loved what I felt.

"Like Pizarro in his glass coffin," I said. She stared at me. I practiced an odd sort of courtship. "I read about that somewhere," I said.

"Was that for a class?"

"No, I think it was in Peru. Pizarro stole so much gold he needed another life to spend it."

"Another life?" she said.

"In the Andes," I said, "where he never found Machu Picchu, and the maidens of the sun. That would take another life."

"This life is enough," she said. She looked at me. "Would you like to walk?"

We walked along foggy streets, or I should say I drifted beside her. Damp cement lay pale where we stepped. The light opened and took her in. We strode long blocks of silence, and then she spoke about the oldest house in her town, the oldest woman, the river. She told how floods came and everyone gathered to watch the bridge go down. As we walked, the sidewalk tapered so narrow, my hand almost brushed her hand.

Once that year, I sat alone in the corner while a party blurred the room with blue smoke. Music drenched the air so loud it seemed to move visibly past me, the beat like the ribs of a groggy fish gliding through the deep, and pounding dancers' feet against the floor. People ate smoke and pills, and grew dizzy and danced, falling, in couples or alone, about the house, until the night tamed nearly everyone, and I sat on the couch listening. Sometime after midnight I heard the record player, finally quieted by the late hour, singing an old song:

> Must I bow down like the willow?
> Must I wait and never know
> How you came to light upon me,
> Ease me down with a touch of snow?

Then the guitar braided something silver in the air, a tender web. I thought of Vera, wondered why I stayed alone. I thought how her house

on a back street bowed under moss and lichen. I remembered her turning
at the doorway to go in, with raindrops touching her hair the way I would.

It seems to me now that the immensity of my longing, without touch,
meant I never saw her, never knew her. I invented a companion with her
name, and visited my invention—I, the man of words and wishes, the puritan in Eden.

After a time, she trusted me, or shared in this invention, and I took her to
the path at the coast, where fog tasted pungent as a meal, where the spruce
tree stood above a fire my hands kindled in the bluff thicket's room.

"This is the life," I said, spreading my hands to the fire. She had taken
off her shoes to warm her feet. She looked at me. Then she looked down.

"This is the life," she said. She leaned back, rolling her coat for a pillow.
She put her hands behind her head. I went for more wood.

When the tide ebbed, we gathered mussels in the rock pool between
breakers. She laughed when a wave caught her, staggered. An animal run
down the beach could solve cold. In the fire, the blue shells opened and we
ate. Creatures of that place, we nibbled at the sea—salt, mussel, and sand.
That made a tough meal. I did not yet know to add butter and wine.

Time passed, Vera found a more ready companion, and I was on my own
without a real goodbye. I drove to the coast, the mountains. I was alone
again, pure and often miserable. And then one night, with my roommate
Paul, I stood in front of the women's dorm and shouted, "Does anyone want
to go to the beach tonight?" Faces appeared at the windows, and then disappeared. But one girl came dancing out across the dark. Her name was May.
And we three drove the sixty dark miles to the Rabbit Hole, threaded the
trail by starlight, gathered wood, laughing in the light of the driftwood fire.

Later, I remember how she cried, how her head tilted back. She had
moved to a house of her own. I sat on her porch the first day we all spun
forward without Martin Luther King.

"I loved that man," she said. "I loved him, that's all."

Inside, the box of the television talked and talked. Men in black and white told the facts. What could we do without Dr. King, his particular dream that had carried us like old music?

When summer came I gave May a basket and took her to gather blackberries between the wolf pens and the river. A certain professor loved wolves, loved to sit in a chair in the deep grass and study them. His research subjects dozed in the sun.

All around their pens, in the abandoned orchard, blackberries were thick, a dark haze of purple in the sunlit leaves and arching vines. May and I worked the perimeter of the thicket, fingering thorns aside to step in close. She stood beside me, reaching like a dancer, with purple on her mouth. Rose vines climbed an apple tree. Grass swayed in the aisles of the orchard, where everything grew free as the seasons ripened—cherries, hazelnuts, apples and pears, the quiet chant of crickets in the flattened grass.

"Do you see that wolf watching us?" she said. "He watches by looking away." She had settled in the grass. She picked twigs and thorns from her basket of dark berries, ate one.

"That's probably how he hunts," she said, "by looking away until he is very close." The sun had dropped low. My hand raised a purple glove to shield my eyes.

She was too beautiful for me to approach. I moved on. One night, I invited a girl, Eva, to *Bullitt*, with Steve McQueen. This was a brutal beginning, but Eva didn't seem to mind. Then there was a dance, and I invited her. After the dance, we drove the long road burrowing through mountains to the trail, took a candle down along the corridor of roots and leaves. This place had to speak my story to the women I met. I had become the spruce tree at the end, upright without a word.

In my den in the bluff thicket, I built fire and her hair shone. I stood above her to add wood to the flames, and my shadow leaped against the trees. She pointed at that, and I turned to look over my shoulder. That night in two sleeping bags, we watched the stars.

One morning, helicopters rattled over the campus, and the National

Guard troops trotted along 13th Avenue in squads bristling with guns. Bands of students roved with linked arms and signs and shouts. Guards stood in silhouette on the roof of the music building, rifles at ready. The black rectangle, a flag's ash, marked the street. We circled the campus in my battered VW bug, dodging the thickest action for a way in, finally slipping up 18th to park at the Pioneer Cemetery. Wind moved in the fir trees. The plots bloomed with lilac and wild rose. We heard chanting, like distant insects, sirens.

"How can I get back to my room?" she said.

"Let's wait here," I said. The city swirled around us like television.

I lived alone, I walked the streets at night, climbed trees in the cemetery to feel the pull of the wind. But I was learning how to be a friend, though often an awkward one.

When I first met Bonnie, I saw how she stood small, close to earth the way a child stands, but her wise face loomed up. She knew how to get by, and she knew life took more than getting by. Her smile made poverty nothing, a story to tell, a puzzle to solve. Her humor could tame the riddles of work and hunger, but not of love.

One morning she appeared with a cloth knotted around her hand and blood at the cuff. Midnight, she said, her boyfriend taunted and raved, bragging about his conquests of other women, and in fury she stabbed an ice pick through her own palm.

I took her through the mountains, down the path to the spruce tree. The wind brought fog up, and the afternoon billowed gently over us. We built fire, shared bread, waited for dark, slept in hollows apart. Stars dimmed. The net of spruce limbs gathered overhead as daylight came. The strength in her small face at dawn held a light I had never seen.

The long drive back to town was filled with friendly quiet. Trust, honor, survival. Then I was alone again.

Vera, May, Eva, Bonnie. Of these four women, I fought past fear to share a kiss with one, and we married. I thought a kiss was a contract: I must marry the one I kiss. . . . I must do the right thing. In a letter home, a week after the wedding, I confided to my parents that I wished I were alone again. "Did I do the right thing?" I don't remember that they ever wrote back. One of the big silences.

Years later, after my brother had died, and my marriage had ended, I was sitting with my father after we had taught a workshop at the coast together.

"Oh, Daddy," I said, "it's hard for me these days. I meet a woman, and it's good for a time, and then something happens, and it ends. There's a lot of blaming, and I don't know what went wrong. And then I meet someone else, and this hard pattern happens again."

"It sound great!" he said.

"It does?"

"Just great. Keep on "

I realized there was something I had wanted to ask for twenty years.

"Daddy, do you remember that day just before I left for college? Do you remember what you said to me about women?"

"What did I say?"

"You said that when you went to college, when you were with women, they trusted you to do the right thing."

"That's right," he said. "They did."

"And what's the right thing?"

"Why, anything!" he said. "Sometimes you turn away, and sometime you dive right in. Why, I remember my first girlfriend, Cozy Allen. When I went to visit her house, her mother would take her knitting and hustle right upstairs so we could be alone. I remember the petting parties. . . ."

"Daddy!" I said. "I thought you meant the 'right thing' was respect, restraint."

"Oh no," he said. "Where did you get that idea? Fantastic. The right thing is the human thing. You feel, and you act. Of course you respect. That's part of doing the right thing. But life is for action."

"Why didn't you tell me all this then?"

"I thought you knew, my friend."

## THE ROAD TO PARIS

The summer of 1969 our parents decided to go to Europe early in the spring, with our sisters, and the plan was that Bret and I would join the clan when school ended. By a stroke of luck, the giant duffel bag I had so carefully packed got left in the car in our haste at the Portland airport, and so I landed in London with a small backpack containing passport, sleeping bag, camera, journal, and my recorder. My brother had about the same, so we bought a few shirts, socks, and a few pairs of underwear, and we were ready to travel light and loose.

After a few weeks with the family—in London, then Scotland, and Ireland—they flew home, and my brother and I were on our own. I can't remember how it was decided, but our plan was to split up in Dublin, ramble separately, and then meet at the youth hostel in Paris two weeks out, and take it from there together.

I'm not clear where Bret went, but I rented a bike in Dublin and headed west without a plan. I remember falling asleep tipsy beside a haystack in a field. I remember the sign on a one-lane country road directing me to Lilliput. I remember stopping at a pottery studio where the artist, seeing my bike and realizing I would never buy a thing, was about to shut her door to me but then thought again and said, "Well, love, who knows? Maybe someday you'll come back in a Jag."

Just to show her, I bought a cup, and carried it in my backpack, perversely, for the next thousand miles.

As the time for our rendezvous in Paris approached, I crossed the Irish Sea to Holyhead, and hitched east through the Welsh collieries, then through Sheffield, past the great Chalk Horse on the hill, and into London. From there I caught a ride to Canterbury, Dover, across the channel to Calais, and up that road to the sign that said Paris south, and Köln north.

For four hours I stood on the west shoulder of that highway, waiting for a ride to Paris. I wondered where my brother had been, whether he was as stingy as me—almost fasting, but feasting on the scene, afraid the money would run out, but famished for this beautiful freedom.

As I began to wilt in the heat, on a whim I crossed the road. "I'll just try for five minutes," I told myself. I stuck out my thumb, and the first northbound car hit the brakes and stopped just beyond me. Then a second car stopped. Two cars, both packed with kids my age, traveling together.

"We can, maybe, fit you," said a lanky boy in a linen shirt. With one glance to the south, I picked up my pack and ran to the car. They folded me in somehow, I on a boy's lap, my pack in my arms, and we set out. So installed, I was facing the rear, and I watched the road recede. What had I done? I had betrayed my brother's trust, that's what. I tried to console myself with the thought that he would have done the same—four hours! But it wasn't working.

Just then, I could see the second car, behind us, was smoking, then sprouting flames. I shouted, pointed, and everyone started talking in multiple languages. Our driver stared in the rearview mirror, swerved and corrected, and pulled off the road. Doors open, we all rolled out of the car, tumbled to the ground, and stood up running toward the burning car. The driver of that car was out, a girl, had her hands in the air, and was screaming "Ma voiture! Ah, Papa!" They had the lid up over the rear engine in flames, and were throwing dirt on the fire. Once we all pitched in, we got it out. But the car—"Kaput." "Morte." "Shagged." In the soot on the raised hood—the "boot," one called it—the French boy traced with his finger the word "F-I-N." The end.

Who were these people? What was I in? A girl began speaking very fast in French, others answered in German, and something else—Danish? It seems there was a distant relative living nearby. We could ferry everyone there in two trips with the other car. I said I'd wait for the second trip, thinking I had to think this through.

By the time the car came back for the rest of us, I had settled the matter. My responsibility to my brother was to live, to find things to tell him, to divide and conquer the world. We would always have plenty of time to share our stories somewhere down the road.

"We 'ave found a big maison," said the driver. "Come." We all piled in, and in twenty minutes were somewhere at the ragged edge of Lille, a dark three-story house, where the lone resident, someone's ancient aunt, was thrilled to have us. She had one word of English, and loved to say it to me over and over, as she poured me a glass of wine, then another.

"Beautiful," she said. "Beautiful." The red wine flowed. I thought one last time of my brother. "Beautiful."

I didn't see my brother for two months, until the day before our flight home. We connected in Amsterdam. I don't remember what he said about our plan to meet in Paris. Instead, he told me about the red-light district.

"They have an actual red light," he said, "and a woman sits in a glass case, like a mannequin." He told me we had missed Woodstock, the big one. I never learned where he had been. We did not spread out a map and compare our travels. I sensed he had a secret hoard he would not share with me.

"It's just so great to be together again," he said. So we went to a screening of *The Graduate*, with subtitles, stayed up all night talking about what we would do when we got home, and barely made the plane.

## ONE OF THE SILENCES

Back in Eugene, college was a continuous high—even the dark days were thrilling, because they were my own. I could walk the streets by night, brooding, or run ecstatic hills at dawn. I didn't have to get myself back down or up to an even keel when something in the world swept me away. My family didn't need to be reassured, I thought, and neither did I.

I remember a time when the family came to Eugene to visit. Bret and I piled into the car, like the old days—me on the left in the back, and Bret on the right, with Kit between us, and Barb between the folks up front, our father at the wheel. As we drove around town looking for a restaurant for dinner, I was babbling away about all kinds of things that had been happening. In my rush, I reported a recent dream that "my family was holding me at gunpoint. . . ." I went rattling on. This dream for me was just one more wonder, a curiosity that was part of the whole crazy experience of life. It didn't mean anything in particular. The movie of each day and night was brilliant with a sense of the new. But gradually, as I babbled, I became aware that the car had grown silent.

"Where shall we eat?" our father said flatly, as he cruised along Franklin.

Silence. Our mother would not say a word. I didn't get it, fool that I was. We drove around and around—west on 11th, north on Onyx, back east on 7th. Finally, I suppose, we found a place, and glumly ate. That part I don't remember.

It wasn't until later, years later, I figured out what was happening. Our mother, and perhaps everyone in the car, had been stunned by my few syllables about the dream. My dream was accusing them, they thought. My dream meant I didn't want them to hold me back, they thought.

I just thought it was a dream, and that talk in their company was the greater truth, and should be honored as the truth. This was life, and a dark dream was a rich curiosity in the midst of learning.

## COLLEGE

What was college for? My brother's three years at the University of Oregon, and my four—what academic residue remains, and what proportion of overall education did the classroom offer?

If I try to answer by documentary evidence, all I have is a sifting of test fragments. This from my brother's final in History 203, administered on June 4, 1968:

Identify and give the significance of the following (30 min.)

Zimmerman telegram
Nye Committee
Wagner Act

Dr. Townsend
Reconstruction Finance Corporation

Or from the more affective side, my brother's final in English 203, on June 6, 1968:

> Discuss the importance of 2 of the following scenes for their dramatic significance in the tragedy. Deal with theme, imagery, characterization to justify your selection (45 min.):
>
> Lear's testing and evaluation of his daughters' love
> The storm scene
> Lear's arraignment of Goneril and Regan in the farmhouse scene
> The arrest, trial and punishment of Gloucester

When I open one of several remaining examination books from those days, written by my brother in his furious scrawl, I witness him seeking to prove his ability to integrate reading and lecture and his own thought in order to snare that A- in American History 203.

> The pamphlet *Roosevelt, Wilson, and the Trusts* delineates, in various parts, some of the reasons for this trend. Among them were matters concerning efficiency—steel, for instance, need be heated only once if a huge combination of companies could carry the whole process of steel production from ore to a finished product, say a railroad tie.

"A railroad tie"? The whole ritual of the final calls for concision. Haste makes a mishmash of deep thought. But study in tragedy, historic trends, and economic imperatives served, in my experience, as understory to the real education in one's college years. Friendship with an idea could go beyond the semester. Unsolved enigmas in class could become a quest in the mountains. What was college for? Classes in subjects invited subjective thought beyond school. Tragedy in Shakespeare could be subplot to one's own life struggles, sorted by starlight for a midnight meditator seated on a stone in the Pioneer Cemetery on campus.

Bret was an excellent student—curious, attentive, persistent. Any teacher would be lucky to have him in class. At the same time, I remember him telling me that he began to see disturbing parallels between the initiation rituals he was studying in anthropology class, and the treatment of students by faculty in the Anthro Department. I remember one of my own friends recounting the extracurricular activities of a particular faculty member among his female students. After her own bedding by him, she said, her eyes were opened, and she was certain she could count over thirty conquests by the same man. "And he wasn't that good in bed," she said. "Took three minutes—after all his talk to get me there. Office hours. Tutorials. 'Getting deeper into the text' with me. What a letdown."

My own experience was of a sweet intersection of books and moonlight, of formal classes and cutting out to wander in the mountains, taking time to prepare on a forest trail for the sociology take-home final we all knew would consist of a single question: "What is the nature of man?"

I remember going to see one of my teachers in his office. I don't remember the class, or our topic, but I do remember I had fallen behind. As he earnestly explained to me what I would need to do in order to pass the class, my gaze kept drifting over his shoulder to a poster on the wall. It showed Joan Baez with two Hispanic beauties, sitting close together on a couch with their bare legs provocatively crossed. The smiles on their faces were brimming with welcome. And under the photo were the words:

> Las muchachas dicen que sí
> a los muchachos que dicen que no.

Thanks to my rudimentary Spanish, I got the gist: Girls say yes to boys who say no. Hey, I'd probably say no to the draft, so I guess that must mean I had a chance with the *muchachas*.

Sensing that I wasn't paying attention, the professor turned to glance at the poster. "Yes," he said, "they are beauties, aren't they?"

There was a proverb in those days that I first encountered where it was scratched into the wall of the third-floor men's room in the library: "Reality is just for people who can't handle their drugs." I didn't do drugs, but I could apply the sentiment: "Classes are for people who don't know how to learn from life." Or "Grades are for people who can't measure learning's personal satisfactions." Or "College is a rehearsal for the later drama of work vs. life."

When I look through the big sheaf of Peace Corps information my brother saved (he never applied but kept the forms), the potential applicant is advised:

> Dear Friend:
> Peace Corps training . . . that probably sounds like some vague, academic ordeal which must be hurdled before one becomes a full fledged Volunteer. That's part of what it is. Training programs are also volatile, spontaneous things which must be altered often and quickly to meet new needs. . . .

That describes for me my own approach to study in college: rigorous, but infinitely flexible, capricious even, in pursuit of that sweet spot where the young body, the fertile mind, an array of classes, and the intuition of each day's dawn conspire together to design the experience of learning.

Though an English major, I took folk dance, Japanese architecture, ceramics, clarinet, jewelry-making, and camp cookery (fifteen geology majors and me, making mock apple pie with Ritz crackers and cinnamon). In the library, I was as likely to hunker down with a subject found by chance as by assignment: photographs of Atget . . . pearl divers of Japan . . . Samoan proverbs . . . indigenous ironworkers of Nigeria. The point was to fashion a personal integration of all temptations to the learning mind—some prescribed, and many simply found, created, dreamed.

The trick was to be ever vigilant for the spark of true learning—in a book, a professor, an idea—or separate from school to be fully awake to a sensation, to a stab of thrilling fear, to the wild chance to make something out of nothing, to a tenacious dream.

## LOTTERY NIGHT

When my brother was in elementary school, he composed a set of maps and letters made to look like archival pages from the Civil War. These include a letter from Robert E. Lee to Abe Lincoln, which concludes, "I am doing some plans for attack right now. How I wish the war had never started." And a letter of surrender from Lee to Ulysses S. Grant, which concludes, "P.S. You're a fine man."

From an early age, he took a great interest in the possibilities of choosing friendship over war. In his mind, he could traverse the vast distance between the two.

Remember those days of the draft and Vietnam: the power of the U.S. government as Old Testament Abraham, willing to sacrifice his sons? The draft sought young men for sacrifice in jungle war. When you looked at a military recruitment poster, you didn't need to be on drugs to see the death's head behind that scowl of the old man aiming his finger at the heart: "Uncle Sam Wants You!" If you read the fine print, there was an option out: "Conscientious Objector: You are opposed on moral or religious grounds to participation in war in any form. You will need to prove the sincerity of your beliefs."

The Draft Board sent each eligible young man a Selective Service card. This little scrap of paper was to be carried at all times, and treated with tremendous respect. According to the notice accompanying my card, I was informed that if I altered the card in any way, I could get up to five years in prison, or a fine up to $10,000, or both. In those days, that was more than the cost of a college degree, and took longer. These figures we could understand. But for a slip of paper?

I have a copy of a document my brother gave me, based on a student poll at Berkeley: "Out of those who will not go in if drafted 60% will leave the country, and 31% will go to jail."

Against this backdrop, on the night of December 1, 1969, the U.S. government held a televised lottery to determine which young men should go to the killing fields in Vietnam. My brother was living with half a dozen friends in an old house on East 12th. That house was the place to be for a party, either dark or festive, and clearly the place to be for this one.

Anyone alive in those days may remember the surreal drama of U.S. congressman Alex Pirnie reaching into a cage to pull out the first of 366 numbered balls (leap-year birthdays got no slack). In his heavy black, mad-scientist glasses, he looked at the ceiling, to assure us he wasn't hand-picking a favorite.

No one in the room was visibly breathing. Bret, Chuck, Bill, Brian, Roger, Jake, and me. The options were on the table: if you got a low number, you went to Nam, to prison, or to Canada. Or, as Bret reminded everyone, you could apply for C.O. status.

"Yeah, yeah, Stafford. Easy for you. Your dad was one. You might get it, but I'm a lousy atheist. No chance."

"Shhh. He's picking. . . ."

I don't remember who got what number, besides the fact that my brother and I had numbers considered high enough by all prophecies we heard to escape the call. We were not in reach of the draft that year. The others, each found some way to step aside—student deferment, followed by deft maneuvers available to the college grad. Bret did apply for C-O status: Conscientious Objector. On his ride in the special army bus from Eugene to Portland, the young men with him got so rowdy, chanting, swearing, swaying—that the driver pulled over and refused to go on. Bret didn't get to Portland until after dark, but he was there to face the board on Warner Milne Road in Oregon City the next morning. (The name of that road, somehow, is a knife in my memory, never to be forgotten.) They really worked him over, called him a coward, said that just because his daddy got off didn't mean he had a free ride. But Bret stood firm, and in the end, with a lot of grumbling, they gave him C.O. status.

When I came of age in October 1967, I registered for the draft. My draft card, which I was to carry with me at all times, specifies that I am five feet, nine inches tall, I weigh 145 pounds, and I can be identified by a two-inch curved scar in my left palm (the result of a tricycle accident at age three). I remember thinking, *They need to know about that scar so they can identify my body on some battlefield.*

When my turn came, I filled out my C.O. application in a feverish all-nighter, making wild intuitive guesses about the doctrines of the Brethren Church where our mother's father had preached, and in the morning sent in the form. Then I went for draft counseling to my old minister, Reverend Jim. He was working at a small church in Tigard then, and he welcomed me warmly. I told him about Bret's harrowing passage on Warner Milne Road.

"That's tough," he said. "But I've heard it can be like that." When I asked for his support in preparing for my own showdown with the Draft Board, he was eager to help. I showed him a copy of my application, and without hesitation he began to tear my reasoning apart. Had I ever really thought about these things, he asked, or was I just assuming I had a pass because my father had a pass, and now my brother, if barely? What about someone attacking my house—am I serious that I wouldn't pick up a gun to defend myself? What kind of love was that?

"If someone put a gun to your brother's head," he said, "would you just stand idly by? Don't you love him? Doesn't love require action? Just because Jesus said the meek shall inherit the earth, does that mean you can chicken out on those you love? What is love, anyway, if it's not the courage to fight for what you love?"

This went on for a good hour. I broke into a sweat, looked down at what I had written on the form.

"Don't look at that form," he said. "Look inside. I'm not interested in what your grandpa thought. What your daddy thought. I need to know what you think. Let's hear it. Or you know what? I want you to go home and think about all this. Come back here in a week and you'd better have some things figured out, or you're in trouble."

Deeply discouraged, I went back to Eugene, talked for the first time with my brother in detail about these matters. He asked hard questions, too. And I had to start from scratch.

The next week, when I sat down with Reverend Jim, I tried to explain another way to do this life than war.

"I don't know what I would do if someone threatened my brother," I said, "or anyone I love—or anyone, really. I probably would take up a weapon if that happened. Even a club. Anything. I'd get as crazy as the next guy if something like that came down. But that's not where we are with this. We are attacking a far country. We are bringing danger to them. Their response is to take up weapons to defend themselves. I can't stop that. The president isn't going to listen to me. But that's not really the point here. The point is that the draft is asking me if I—one person, this one person—will take up a gun and follow orders to go kill someone in Vietnam. And my answer to that question is no. I don't believe that's the best action, ever. Not just this war. No war. For me, no war, ever, anywhere."

I carried on like this, and he let me. I found holes in my own thinking, sometimes, and had to circle back. My conversation with my brother, and then this conversation, were the first times I had really considered the far-reaching implications of one person's action, or inaction. It had all been abstract before. Now it was about deciding, in the face of a skeptic, what I had to do. I fought my way through all the questions he threw at me.

Finally, Revered Jim's face softened. "Okay," he said. "That's enough. You probably won't convince anyone on the Draft Board that you are right, but you can show them that your beliefs are your own. They can either ask the taxpayers to fund your time in prison, or they can follow the law and grant you C.O. status. I suspect that's what they'll do."

I got up to go, and he said, "I'm sorry I was so hard on you in our first meeting. I had to do that. I had to be the Draft Board, and really attack. I hope you can see that was an expression of my respect for you, my love for you and your family."

"I only wish," I said, "my brother had come first to you."

When I appeared before my Draft Board, I was raring for a fight. But to my disappointment, the four men behind the table muttered quietly among themselves, and then one of them said, "You're I-O, kid. We're done. You can tell the next man in the lobby he's up."

I still have that card, marked I-O, full conscientious objector status, signed by Frank Belcher, member of the local board. After my long preparation, this dénouement was a drop. But I stepped outside the building and realized a subtle gray fog—my fear of my government's power—had burned away. I was free.

Years later, I found a poem my brother had written in those days. Eventually, he would go to Canada, even though he had been granted C.O. status. He did not feel right being in a country that made war. But in the poem, he dealt with the problem as our father might have—seeing the situation by the liberal half-light of the imagination:

> The Pentagon self-consciously
> slinks below ground
>
> And arises a starfish on some
> sunny beach
>
> To be gazed at in Wonderment
> by a curious child.

My brother was the curious child, but he was a soldier, too. He took his orders from some interior general our childhood had made inside his mind. "All the little sputniks," his poem says, "are alone."

## DODGIN' THE DRAFT

Shortly after facing the Draft Board, I had to take one of my wild circuits far from school, from family, from everyone in order to get my bearings in the world. It was as if, for me, one vision quest in a life was not enough—not the water tower, the roads of Europe, or any of my other raids on mystery. I had to have another.

Waking one morning before spring break, I realized that the city of Victoria, on Vancouver Island in British Columbia, beckoned. From the day my brother and I had plunged into the primitive infinity of the Provincial Museum there as children, the city always had honor in my mind. Our father was doing some kind of workshop in Port Townsend. I could go that far with him, then ride my bike west to Port Angeles, cross to Victoria by ferry, and come back through the San Juan Islands, catching the train for Eugene at Mount Vernon, Washington.

I asked my brother, but school was getting serious for him—history, geography, sociology.

"But it's spring break," I said.

"Doesn't matter."

So off I went. We made it to P.T. on a Sunday afternoon, and I unloaded my bike from the family car, wished our father a good class, and headed west. Just barely caught the last ferry at P.A., and landed in Victoria long after dark. From previous visits, I knew where the park was, and even the thicket that would be my hidden bed. When I had been there at twelve, that hollow was my fort. Now it was my camp.

In the morning, bewhiskered, walking my bike along Fort Street, I stepped into a bakery for a muffin. An earnest girl behind the counter took one look at me after hearing my American speech, and burst out, "Ooh, man, are you dodgin' the draft?"

"No, just biking around."

She lowered her voice. "You can tell me," she whispered. "We have a safe house for your kind."

"What kind of safe house?"

"Just a house with beds and food," she said, "for friendly travelers like yourself. No charge."

That last bit got my attention. I took the address, and agreed to appear there at dusk.

That night, it wasn't long into the dinner of soup and bread that the real agenda surfaced. I was placed at the head of the table with Beck; the girl to my left; long-haired Dylan—a boy my age—to my right; and Joe, the studious man in his late twenties opposite me who seemed to be in charge.

After Beck gave a long grace, which included my need for guidance from on high, we raised our heads and I asked Dylan to please pass me the bread.

"Have you give serious consideration to asking Jesus Christ to be your personal savior?" he said, without moving.

"Ummm. Sort of." I said.

"This might be a good time to do so," said Beck. "We have time, and maybe this is what brought you to Victoria today, and to this house."

I looked back and forth from Beck to Dylan, and then at Joe.

"Dylan," he said, "you're doing fine, but I think I heard our guest ask for some bread. Why don't you send it around for all of us? Now, go on. . . ."

For the next hour, Beck and Dylan gave me every possible chance, with a variety of questions, warnings, and even a few veiled threats, to take this occasion to heart. Joe let them work. The soup grew cold.

I had a ring on my right ring finger, and in my discomfort I began fiddling with it, taking it off, putting it on, taking it off and setting it down. I felt like I was before the dark incarnation of Reverend Jim again.

Finally, Joe gentled his minions. "Tell me about that ring," he said. "It seems to be important to you. What's the story of the ring?"

I held it up, then on impulse handed it to Dylan. "I made it," I said. "It's cast from a bay leaf, rolled into a circle. It's silver. There's a girl—a woman I'm thinking of giving it to."

In silence, the ring was passed around. When it came back to me, Joe said, "My friends, I think we have done our work tonight. Shall we give our traveler his rest?"

I put on the ring, wrapped my bread in my red bandana, they showed me to a room upstairs, and in the morning, before first light, I was out of there.

## CARNABY STREET

When I look back at my brother's life, I see a pattern I did not see then: he would go to a far place, would strive there for an augmented identity beyond what he could be with us, and then he would return and try to be that person here. Maybe everyone does this, growing up, negotiating the essential contradictions of distance, growth, rejection, loyalty, identity—and the chameleon soul.

Several summers after our family trip to Europe, Bret went there alone. I learned later he went on a one-way ticket. One of his big jumps beyond us. He stayed in London under circumstances I never fully understood. There was a residence of some kind, with a charismatic landlord. Bret fell under the spell of this person, as he had fallen under the spell of Alan Watts through his reading, or, earlier, the spiritual vocation of the pacifist, from our parents' teaching. In this case, Bret came home wearing a set of new beliefs that he tried to tell us. My memory for detail is vague, perhaps as a result of my inability to truly attend to my brother, or of his inability to convey his new guru's teachings to us, back in Oregon, and I too firmly set in our Stafford ways.

In any case, there came the morning when Bret announced he wanted to show us his new outfit from Carnaby Street. We knew this would be mod, irreverent, a firm departure from our Midwest family custom. He carried a package into the bathroom down the hall, and we waited, my sisters and I, in the living room. It was such a setup, I wonder now that none of us saw what was coming.

When Bret emerged, in a nubby, wide-cut jacket and bell bottoms, with a flowered tie and shiny shoes, we laughed. We giggled, rolled on the floor, cackled helplessly.

I see him there: his hands hanging down, his face fallen, pleading eyes.

He went back into the bathroom, and we never saw those clothes again. *We didn't mean it! We were sorry!* We begged him to wear the clothes. We told him a torrent of truths and lies and wishes to get him to show us, tell us, be with us in the spirit of where he had been and what he had learned.

Clearly, he was converted to something there, but I never learned what it was, because we laughed him back into silence, conformity. He went to London and dressed himself in a way he discovered on his own, under the spell of the place and the time and his distance from us—early 1970s. And then we killed what he had started to try to be.

Years later, I stood before the Sacred Coffee shop, just off Carnaby Street in London, before it opened, and I thought of my brother, his dreamtime alone in that place. It had rained. I walked empty streets, drank the morning light, and felt the tone of gathering bustle: ale barrels trundled into Shakespeare's Head tavern, and trucks with workers everywhere unloaded great bundles of clothing, a woman with a dozen suits in wavering plastic over her arm. The Royal Mail truck made its rounds. I stood a long time beside an office building with a sign: This was the site of the house of William Blake. Blake went the distance with his wondrous dreams, but my brother kept his hid.

## THE SWEETBRIAR

I thought I really had it made when I got a summer job as busboy at the Sweetbriar Inn, a half-hour bike ride from home. The maître d' and my patron, Dale Thorne, told me early on that he had been identified in some competition as "the third best-dressed man in Portland." What kind of contest would determine that, and what kind of man would proclaim he had come in third? Well, you get the idea. Dale was a tiny man who drove a huge Caddy. The chef was a man named Cliff, who traded steak dinners to the waitresses in return for drinks and announced to us busboys late one night that he was married to the former Miss Scappoose. The owner was a high-anxiety character named Mr. Kronar, who would fly into a rage if one of us mistakenly put the gold-rimmed plates through the dishwasher instead of washing them with speedy tenderness by hand. One night, the dishwasher, having decided to quit, took outside the long aluminum pole used to put up and take down letters, and changed the words on the marquee that faced the freeway to "KRONAR'S COOKING OH SHIT." Then he stashed the pole, flung his apron to the kitchen floor, threw us all a wicked grin, and took off. We waited for the volcano, and it wasn't long before a customer reported to Mr. Kronar what he'd seen on the marquee, and Mr. K was in the kitchen in the most severe rage I had ever witnessed. Smoke seemed to pour from his ears, and fiery percussion from his mouth.

What a great night! This was my world. Dale sent me in the Caddy for more lemons when we ran out, or romaine, or croutons. I would cautiously steer the cruise liner of a car out of the parking lot, then open her up on the straightaway. One night, a guest in the inn fell in the shower, and I was dispatched to drive the poor man to the hospital.

"Do not say you are sorry," Dale told me. "Say nothing about the accident. Just get him to the E.R. and bring my car back before the dinner rush."

I was groomed for this B-grade version of the good life, Dale's pet, filled with stories of trumped-up menus for naïve customers. I watched Dale close in on a young couple obviously new to eating out, maybe even a first date, dithering over their menus. He would sweep up to their table, pluck the menus from their hands, and say, "Why don't you just let me feed you." The young swain, afraid to resist in front of his date, said nothing. Dale brought a series of our most expensive dishes to their table, then dropped the bill and went into hiding until they had paid and were gone.

In this rich milieu, I was trained to make Caesar salads on a little cart beside a customer's table, crushing garlic in cracked ground pepper and whisking in the egg, lemon, and oil before tossing in the romaine—broken, not sliced with a knife. For some reason, this distinction was a very big deal.

One evening there was to be a rehearsal dinner in the back banquet room. Carrying a tray of ice waters into that boisterous crowd, I made my way along the table inhabited primarily by drunken men a few years older than me. With a shock I recognized the bride sitting at the head of the table beside a red-faced boy—the groom. It was the lovely Lark. She was the daughter of a car dealer in our town. She was a thoughtful person, known as "a brain" in our school. A writer. Modest. Kind. And she had been, for a brief time, my brother's girl. They were clearly meant for each other. Wasn't her poem printed opposite his story in *Mainsheet*, the Lake Oswego High School literary magazine in 1965? When you closed the magazine, her words about Auschwitz and his about a mine disaster were together, face to face.

"Hey," said one of the revelers, holding up a white napkin that had fallen into a pool of ketchup on his plate, "this looks like one that's been used!"

Was I getting this right—he was making a joke at the bridal dinner by comparing his napkin to a bridal sheet? Lark had clearly fallen into the wrong crowd. She should be with my brother, more in keeping with her creative and sensitive nature. I almost dumped the tray of waters on that reveler's head, met the level gaze of the bride, who, in that moment, recognized me as Bret's little brother, and I fled the room.

## CHILD OF LUCK

In college, I lived by whim. Waking in the morning, I did what came to mind. On impulse one Monday dawn I decided to cut class and drive on through campus toward the mountains. I loaded the VW bug with snacks, camera, my hat and walking stick, and headed out. Half a mile south of campus, cruising north along Hilyard Street with the morning rush, I saw a hitchhiker and pulled over, automatically, to offer him a lift. It was my teacher for Western Civ, Mr. Quinn.

"What a coincidence," he said. "You're Mr. Stafford, aren't you? You're in my eight o'clock."

"Ah . . . yeah," I said. "But, actually . . . I'm on my way up the Mackenzie. It's too beautiful for class. No offense."

"I wish I could head that way," he said. "We'll miss you in class, but I can't say I blame you. Just do the reading, and we'll see you on Wednesday."

I dropped him off by Commonwealth Hall, he waved, and I went on my way, east toward the forest. "What a great teacher," I thought.

I drove through Springfield, past the lumber mill, and then took the highway that zigzagged up the valley, fully loaded log trucks thundering past me on the curves, heading for town. Then I was into the canyon, the road steepening toward the Mackenzie headwaters, crossed over at Santiam Junction, and headed west until I came to the turnoff for Whitewater Creek. Seven miles on gravel, skidding on the washboard curves. Left the car at the end of the road and climbed the trail into the grove of huge, old trees. A towhee called, and I could hear my heart thudding as I charged up the slope. At a sun-spangled bend in the trail, I stopped to photograph a young tree at the foot of a shaggy giant Douglas fir. Sunlight had found the young one, featured it there. There was something about the pluck of that sapling under the ponderous old ones that caught my fancy.

Later, in the campus darkroom, I made a print of that image, mounted it on cover stock, and mailed it to our parents. Under the photo I wrote a line from *Oedipus Rex*, the play due to be discussed on the day I missed class: "I am a child of luck."

I realized that when Oedipus utters this line, irony is at work. He does not know what he says, what he is, what he has done, or what is ahead for him. The line is a statement of hope, a moment of confidence.

That was me before the great change.

## "I'VE ASKED MY NEPHEW"

Our Aunt Helen, our mother's older sister, lived alone in our town, and one time she asked me to come by to water her plants when I was home and she was away for a few days. "Especially the geraniums," she said.

Well, I got to doing other things, and then I remembered. When I finally raced to her house and found the hidden key in the flowerpot, a few days late, and opened the back door, I found a note addressed to the next-door neighbor: "Pat, I've asked my nephew to look after things, but he is not always the most reliable, so I appreciate your willingness to keep my dear geraniums alive."

The pots were damp. The house silent. I hid the key and slunk away.

## A WEEK OF HONEY

Somewhere, somehow, my brother met a girl from Michigan, and she showed up in Eugene on a lovely day in spring. I was living in an apartment, upstairs in a house beside the house where my brother lived with his six roommates. Out the window, as I labored on a late paper, I saw my sunlit brother loading his car with camping gear and the winsome lass lending a hand as she skipped from one foot to the other. She danced, and he seemed to be levitating. By the time I got down the stairs to meet her, they were gone.

That was a Friday. The following Wednesday, they showed up at the house to get some food and clean clothes, and then they headed west for the coast. My glimpse of the girl was of a happy beauty who brought a light step and a grin to my brother's life.

"After you make love," he told me later, "it's good to stay with the woman, just stay close. I got up to take some pictures of Smith Rocks, and she got upset. But pretty soon it was good again."

I never heard more about her, and I don't remember her name.

## THIRTEEN CEMETERIES

The goal in college, as I remember it, was to find a class where there was maximum flexibility about how to fulfill assignments, and then to rev your imagination to the max and invent a project that would keep the professor happy and set yourself free.

My own greatest coup in this regard was my proposal for "Introduction to Northwest Folklore." I would survey thirteen rural and remote cemeteries in the high desert country of central Oregon, take photographs, draw maps, record inscriptions on gravestones, and inquire into "the relations between the communities of the living and their dead."

I remember my professor reported receiving one term paper with a joint paper-clipped to the ten rambling pages. A note advised, "I was high when I wrote this. You might want to be high when you read it."

I don't know what my professor was on when he read my proposal (did I mention it involved missing two weeks of class?), but he gave me the nod.

Next thing I knew I was on gravel roads circling and circling the few remnant buildings of the town of Grizzly, south from Madras, searching for the cemetery clearly marked on my USGS topo map. Where was it? Got to be right here. Then I saw it—out there in the wheatfield, no road, an island of history surrounded by this year's golden stand of grain.

I waded through the wheat, studied the worn, sun-silvered boards of the fence left long ago around the plot of a dozen graves, recorded what I saw with my camera and notebook, lay down on a grave to view the sky—long ribbons of thin cloud trailing up from the south.

Then I was driving east on Bake Oven Road, grasshoppers hitting the windshield, seeking the cemetery at Antelope. Then Shaniko, Madras, Redmond, Camp Polk. By the time I got to my last cemetery, out in the northwest corner of the Warm Springs Reservation, I was getting dizzy with it all. I climbed out of the car with my camera. Beyond a screen of trees I could see the graves covered with the bleached remains of toys, trinkets. Out of nowhere, a man with long gray braids appeared.

"You don't want to be here," he said. "Take my word."

## NIGHT VIGIL

My brother was struck down by mysterious pain. Student Health Services could not diagnose his condition. Sent him home to sleep on it. Deeper pain. Finally, a doctor said, "Appendicitis—acute, danger of bursting. It's twisted to the side. You need that out now."

Our parents were far away on a journey. I checked him in, and I waited. It took longer than usual, they told me. Thought they got it in time.

I sat by my brother's bed after the operation. He was out, gone, deep, twitching fitfully. I took his hand, cold.

"Be all right," I whispered. "Please be all right." He was smaller than me, his face drawn, pale. His mouth was slightly open. Shallow breath.

I remembered a story my brother had told about a hike he took alone into the high country east of Eugene. Far from the road, hearing a scuffle, he had left the trail and climbed into a meadow. Two bears were rolling over and over in the lupine, slapping, nipping. He realized it was love, and stood in the shadows, mesmerized. When they rolled in his direction, he got down on his hands and knees, and crept away into a thicket of young hemlock trees.

As I touched my brother's shoulder on the hospital bed, I thought how he had been prepared by that for this. And might he be prepared by this, if he lived, for the best life he might have beyond college, beyond our family, beyond me.

## DUSK AT BLITZEN

Every once in a while my brother and I would light out with half a plan. He might say on a Thursday night, "Señor, let's cut out tomorrow and do the Steens." And off we would go to Steens Mountain in the southeastern Oregon desert. Or I might say, "Señor, I heard about a road in the Ochocos . . . ," and we would be gone from calendar and all expectation but good company and the beauty of surprise.

I remember us in the VW bug we shared, leaving a good road that contoured along the uplands of the Ochoco Mountains northeast from Prineville, and starting down a beckoning track that led into a ravine filled with ponderosa pine.

"This has got to go somewhere," my brother said, as he peered up over the wheel at the descending ruts of the road. "Do you think it will get us back onto Highway 20?"

"That or something better," I said. "We've got our camping gear. What can happen?"

For a time, the track was fine—two good ruts, and no holes deep enough to drop the car and flatten the pan on the hump between them. Then, as often happened, we came to a place where the ruts deepened, and the classic twin questions entered our minds in tandem: (1) could we get through? and (2) if we can't get through, could we get back this way, if we had to? Often, we answered the first question yes, and figured we could deal with the second one, you know, later.

The ravine grew steep, and soon it was clear we would not be climbing back the way we had come, even if we could get our VW bug turned around. The pitch was just too severe. So we picked our way down the road. I remember leaning back in the seat at one point, thinking I could keep the bug from cartwheeling forward. Then the bed of the canyon leveled out, the ground grew damp, and we skirted a patch of cattails that birthed a rivulet our track followed, as the ground opened before us.

There was a cabin of brown pine boards, shingles curling on the roof, but windows still showing shreds of curtain, and the door shut snug. We left the car, tried the knob, and the door swung open. A table, with two chairs pushed back. An old-style kerosene lamp, a few books on a low shelf. A purple velvet coverlet, nibbled along the edge by mice, draped over a short-legged double bed of pine.

It felt holy to be there, as if we were the ghosts of that life come back to find the raveling end of our conversation by lamplight in another century. I remember a tone of close inquiry with my brother there, in whispers as we carefully picked up, turned over, and put down the materials of a life in that house. What happened to these people? How did they live in such a beautifully remote place? What could it all mean? And what about us? What were we for? Would anyone ever study the implements of our life like this?

It was getting dark when we closed the door, and went on down the canyon. Our road disappeared, and we made our way across open ground between old ponderosas, following every downhill hint by guess where the headlights opened before us, until we came to a gate, and beyond the gate a gravel road that led us back to the twentieth century. We had a good, greasy dinner in Redmond before the long, dark run back over the Santiam and down the McKenzie to Eugene.

On a rainy weekend, we hitchhiked to Blue Lake, and walked west to Corbett meadow when the cottonwoods were turning gold. We climbed the Horse Creek trail into the Three Sisters Wilderness, camping beside Separation Creek in a glorious night storm of lightning and rain. We returned to Glass Butte, the mountain of obsidian we had visited as children, in the days when our parents took us by similar half-intention and half-intuition out to the dry country east of the mountains. I remember standing beside Bret where we had walked until we could not see the car behind us. He stood in one rut of the dirt road, and I in the other. He held out his hand for me to be still.

"I can hear my heart," he said. "Just listen."

When I turned my head, I could hear the tendons in my neck crackling, and yes, at the center, my heart was steady and would go forever.

On one of these vagabond transects in eastern Oregon desert country, my brother and I decided we had to see Blitzen, a blue dot identified as a ghost town on one of our older maps. We headed east through Bend to Burns, then south to Frenchglen, and south from Frenchglen on a series of ever simpler roads, until we were barreling along in the Oldsmobile (can't remember the arrangement that freed up the family wheels) on a one-lane dirt track through the sage. I was driving, and we were rattling along at about fifty, trading stories and wild ideas, when my brother suddenly shouted, "Stop!" Without seeing what he saw, I hit the brakes and we went into a long skid through a plume of dust. When the car came lurching to a halt, the front bumper was just pressing against a barbwire gate across the road. He had seen it, I had not. We opened the gate, rolled through, closed the gate, and picked up speed again.

I don't remember much about the town, or what was left of it: a few leaning false-front buildings in weathered pine, and rusted artifacts half-buried in rabbit brush and tumbleweeds. It was dusk by then, and as my brother started up the car, he noticed the fuel tank was just about empty. I had missed that. It was a classic moment: Should we meekly retrace our path for a known distance to a known gas station? Or should we go on, by guess and gamble, to see what might turn up? As I remember the moment, we studied the last gold light across the western rim of the horizon and felt the gathering chill in the air. My brother voted to go back, and I voted to go on. But it might have been the other way around. We traded off as cautionary and loony. At any rate, we decided to go on, and seeing a single light across the desert in a northwesterly direction, I suggested we abandon roads, aim for the light, and make our way through the scattered sage across the open country. This we did.

What followed was a trancelike passage through the gathering dark. Sage blurred on either side, as my brother chose every opening that offered us the general direction of the light. We drove in silence for a time. Stars came on through the windshield. The far light glinted hard, with a tinge of blue. The car bounded over soft ground, as his hands on the wheel swayed back and forth in a kind of dance, and I felt my brother and I were suspended in a little eternity of affection and good luck. The light got no closer. We realized how clear the air must be. You could see forever across the dark earth. The engine hummed, and a coyote flashed away where our headlights swept the gray sage.

## "HOW ABOUT YOU, MR. STAFFORD?"

Where I went to college, buildings were made of brick, windows were framed in aluminum, and desks were whittled and inked with graffiti—sometimes profane, sometimes literary: snippets of poetry inscribed by English majors preparing in advance for an in-class final. You might find the complete text of Sir Thomas Wyatt's "They Flee from Me that Sometime

Did Me Seek" worked into the wood with a blue ballpoint beside a whittled *Venus of Düsseldorf* with orifice enlarged for emphasis.

In such a room, in my first weeks of graduate school, in the Middle English Dialects class designed—I had been told—to wash out the unworthy, I had just sidled into my favorite seat in the shadows of the back row and slouched down to be out of view, almost, of our professor, the imposing Dr. Boren, when he announced, "I have decided I don't want to teach class today." He let several beats of silence pass, to build suspense. Then, "I want one of you to teach today. . . ." There was another beat of silence, as he scanned the room, while, with an almost imperceptible shimmer, each student wriggled lower down, in order to become invisible, and then Dr. Boren magisterially pointed his blunt finger at me and said, "How about you, Mr. Stafford?"

What happened next is a movie I have viewed on the screen of memory countless times: the light in the room turned blue, then gold. I was surrounded by a sphere of fire. A steady, reasonable voice, inaudible to everyone but me, began to explain: "No, that's not how it works, Dr. Boren. I pay tuition so you will read many books so you can tell me what they say so I can be filled with knowledge so I can go forth from this place pretending to understand things I have taken on faith from you." I shivered, hardly able to believe I was standing up. As I walked forward along the right side of the classroom toward the podium, in a trance that had sound effects consisting of a drum roll and the blare of trumpets, and Dr. Boren walked along the left side of the classroom toward my now-empty desk, I experienced a thunderous gestalt change: I realized that the teacher, like a priest, stands between the gods of literature and hapless students. But between the teacher and Geoffrey Chaucer, the Pearl Poet, or the authors of anonymous lyrics from the twelfth century that had ravished my heart—in that space just above my head as I turned to face the class, there was no barrier, no intermediary. I was in an intimate space with the literary voice itself, reporting as if by radio to scattered listeners in the room before me—or, more accurately, below me.

What followed was a living film of our teacher's behavior. How else did I know to do it? I called on students in turn, asked them to read a passage in Middle English, then made comments on their pronunciation. Unforgivable. And my predicament: since Dr. Boren did not call on my fellow students by their first names, and since I was basically a loner, I had to follow his custom.

"Miss Small," I said to a girl in the front row who had long intrigued me, "would you take the first stanza on page 37?"

Perhaps it goes without saying: I lost the possibility of future friends. Miss Small in particular. Who could feel kindly toward a mere student who had the temerity to pretend to be a teacher? But I gained something, too. I left school that day and began to live in the world of pure learning. Never again would anyone stand between me and the poet. We were close companions in a quest for understanding.

I never went back.

## THE WISDOM OF INSECURITY

In college, I got drunk once. At my brother's place, beside the house where I lived in a second-floor apartment, there was wine, and I decided to see what that was all about. I had somehow made it through high school without alcohol—this fit with the family code by which we lived—and through the first two years of college without either drugs or booze. But this time, I was curious. As a festive night swirled about me, and my brother's friends talked and made music, I downed most of that bottle of cheap red. It was bitter, elevating, odd. The next thing I knew, I was in the backyard, on my hands and knees, vomiting. Then I crawled into the backseat of a car someone had abandoned back there. I remember the floor of the car was filled with dry leaves. Maybe there were no windows, and the leaves had blown in from the old maples that lined our street. It was cold. I could not shut off my conscious mind, the mind that kept telling me the obvious: This is not fun. You are helpless. This is boring.

What happened to the myth about drifting off into some kind of sweet delirium? Isn't that what a drugged state promised to offer? It didn't work for me. Perhaps if I had tried often, with the kind of sustained inquiry that I brought to photography, writing, or wandering aimlessly, I might have developed the ability to savor a good drunk. But that night was my only chance, and it closed me down.

I had forgotten one outcome of this experiment with wine until years later I received an angry email from a friend I had forgotten. Out of the blue, he wanted to remind me of my insufferable habit at college parties of bringing my own bottle of "wine," and sipping from it modestly, while others drained their own libations and got drunk. My wine, he found out somehow, was water I had poured into an old empty. I was sipping water, and watching excess unfold all around me.

I do remember one party where this was my disguise. Everyone in that upstairs room got plastered, disappeared into bedrooms, leered toward me with thick perfume, then veered away when I did not respond. Shut out from their deep pleasures, I had what I thought was my own good time.

The writer said he would never forgive me. Perhaps I will never quite forgive myself.

Did my brother drink, drink to excess, do drugs? I don't know. Why don't I know? This was a huge dimension of those days. And yet, somehow the two of us, at the same college and in the same town, were apart, suffering our own binges of loneliness and denial.

I don't remember speaking with him about such things. Maybe when he was at Grinnell, part of the silence was about indulgence there—a drench of beer, or wine, or pot. But he never said a word about that to me. My own experience, and my experience of my brother, was about intoxications of another kind: ideas, questions, places, different ways to live.

In college, someone gave my brother a copy of a book by Alan Watts, and for some years afterward, I heard a lot of philosophy. Fervently, often late at night, my brother would tell me bits and fragments from the teaching of Watts. We didn't understand our own lives, apparently. As Watts explained, through my brother's telling, we had bought into a kind of comfort with security. Personal security was related to military mania for national security. At least that's how the ideas, filtered through my brother, were passed along to me.

One little window I have into his life in those days came from a woman far away who had known my brother when he first came to Eugene. She reports that she sensed his struggle to find his place in the scheme of things. My brother told her, she said, about me, my writing, our father's work. She knew him briefly, she said, but in some elemental way: "He let his soul be known." She also said of him,

> He had a completely open visage. [In my mind] I would see over and over his laughter—his face shook softly and his eyes danced, his Adam's apple bobbing. I am not a writer so I have no words to describe how his total being seemed strung together by the particular levity of the moment. But I think whatever weights he was carrying evaporated in moments like those.

With this report, I think of my brother telling others about his family, about his father, and his brother who shared the father's writing life. I do not think he let his soul be known to me. Maybe the "wisdom of insecurity" was his self-schooled attempt to be free of us. Maybe there was a war in him between a native levity and a self-imposed reticence. I find on a notecard from those years in my brother's hand: "Strange thing: joy and freedom (not somber and melancholy). Wonderful: No longer are we chained to worry about answers; no longer can this world harm us."

I remember one night at the house he shared with the other guys. One was a slender Spanish major. Another a gruff buoyant character, whose idea of the good life was "get a good woman and fuck her every night." Another had taken to riding his bike naked in the wee hours of the morning after a few too many beers at Max's Tavern. And then there was the Presbyterian stalwart, my brother's oldest friend from high school, who looked upon all things with quiet tolerance.

In this mix was my brother, and his Watts-inspired notion of the wisdom of insecurity. My dear brother wanted desperately to believe this wisdom, though it was clearly foreign to his animal need for safety, a sense of confidence, and home.

Why didn't I know then he was setting out on an impossible path?

## "I HAVE YOUR BROTHER"

One morning I was wakened by a phone call from a bail bondsman in Berkeley.

"I have your brother," he said, "and I'll need a thousand dollars to get him out of jail—soon."

"What do you mean?" I said. "My brother is living next door to me here in Eugene. He's probably still asleep."

"Trust me, son," said the voice on the line. "I have your brother. How soon can you get me that grand?"

Turned out, it was true. On a whim, my brother and his housemates, watching the news, had decided to drive down to Berkeley and see what the riots were all about, enter the mix, live the moment. In their innocence, they walked toward the shouting, seething mass of students at the university, got caught in the sweep, and landed in jail.

I can't remember how I got the money—again, it seems the folks were out of town somewhere. I scraped it together, and wired "the grand" to the bail bondsman. A few days later, my brother and his cronies showed up in Eugene, triumphant, veterans of history, for a sliver of time at the center of our generation's dream.

## TWIGGY AT BIG CAMAS

When I was little, when people asked me what I would do when I grew up, without fail I replied that I would be a forest ranger. In my mind this was a green-hatted combination Indian, naturalist, hermit in a cabin with a real fireplace—someone who puttered around in the woods, wearing green.

I never questioned this future, until I chanced to meet a real forest ranger during the fire season of my thirteenth year. I told him my plans, and he replied, "Don't do it, son. It's hell."

I was daunted, and gradually turned to other dreams. I still thought I would live in a cabin in the woods—who would want to live anywhere else?—but my income would not come from the government. At one point, my brother illustrated my dream in an anniversary card he made for our parents. On the cover is an elaborate scene with a total of 138 individuals trees (I counted them), a river, a lake, and a cabin with chimney, smoke, and winding path. The drawing is titled "Kim's Hide-Away in the Cascades (I Hope You'll Invite Me)." I had forgotten the detail associated with my fantasy, but as with many things, my brother paid attention and left a record.

So I fell away from the path of being a forest ranger, but my brother kept the faith. And when he was in college, he began sending applications for summer employment to ranger districts all over. I have a sheet with a listing of sixteen districts in Oregon, Washington, and Idaho. Each has a checkmark beside it. He applied to the National Park Service as well—Yosemite, Yellowstone, McKinley.

Thanks to his persistence, for seven summers, my brother worked for the U.S. Forest Service, repairing trails in the wilderness, doing soil conservation with ax and hoe, staffing recreation areas, and fighting fires. At one point, he had advanced to G4 status, and was earning $2.05 an hour. When he described the work he had done the previous summer on one of his later application forms, he listed "fire fighting on ten fires in Region 6; training—calisthenics every day, hiking with fire packs, practice digging fire line, practice fires, constructing helispots." I remember his crew called that last task "hell-of-a-spots," as the work required bushwhacking to the top of a hill in the middle of nowhere, and cutting down everything in a radius wide enough to allow a helicopter to land.

One summer, early on, I had to drive with my new bride south from Sisters, where we were living, through Chemult where my brother was stationed nearby, at Diamond Lake, and then on to Roseburg for a wedding where a friend of my wife was the bride. We started early so we could have some time to visit with my brother, as it was Sunday, and he was off duty. When we arrived he had lunch ready, and then showed us around. I remember envying the spare simplicity of his life, the beauty of the place, his buoyant independence. My wife used his cabin to put on her fancy dress, as we were running late for the wedding by the time we set out. My brother directed us to a shortcut, an old logging road through the forest that would intersect the main highway down the Umpqua, he said, and save us time. As I glanced at my brother in the rearview mirror, saw his jolly wave, I remember thinking he had it made.

A few miles farther on, as the shortcut road began to deteriorate, as dust filled the car, as my bride began weeping, and peeling off her dusty dress while I drove pell-mell forward, I knew Bret was living the simple life.

There is a photo of my brother on one of many fires. He is sitting in an orchard, somewhere in the apple country of the Okanagan, eating a sandwich. His hickory shirt and suspenders make him look very manly, and the impressive mask of soot across his face proves he's been in the thick of it. In a letter home about that fire, he reports:

> Probably the biggest event was our Lake Chelan, Washington fire.
> It was 25,000 acres, and could have been a lot bigger if the wind
> hadn't started blowing back into the fire and (so we like to think) the
> Umpqua crew hadn't been there. Actually, the Fire Control Officer
> for Region 6, from Portland, said that our crew, in the mad dash
> we made down into the canyon to dig over a mile of fire line in the
> moonlight, had saved about a thousand acres of timber.

In this vocation, he followed our father's legacy from World War II, when Daddy was a pacifist interned in the mountains under the supervision of the Forest Service. Bret carried an eight-foot crosscut saw called a "misery whip" into the wilderness, where chain saws were not allowed, to saw through fallen trees and clear the trails for hikers. He built water-bars to shunt storms from eroding the trails, and practiced what he described to me as the custom of "knock a rock, kick a stick"—clearing trails even as he strode along en route to a work site.

One time my brother reported their trail-maintenance crew had returned to the trailhead to find a small Japanese car that had been left at the end of the road by hikers in the wilderness. The supervisor, a World War II veteran with a deep streak of prejudice, announced to Bret and the other workers, "We'll fix that little rice-grinder." They worked together for an hour to lever a giant boulder into place to keep the car from getting back on the road, then got into their own rig and drove away.

This was one of several times when my brother reported such shenanigans to me with great delight, only realizing in the course of the telling that he had been part of something wrong. I remember his laughter evaporating as he told the story, and how shame set in. "What was I thinking, Señor Mendelphoze?"

The high point of this work seems to have been the two summers Bret was part of the "hotshot crew" at Big Camas station at the top of the Umpqua drainage in the Oregon Cascades. This was an elite team of firefighters dispatched first when a fire flared up to contain the blaze; then they headed on to the next headline fire and let lesser crews mop up the aftermath.

In the spring before his second summer there, his supervisor, Ray Loony, wrote to my brother, listing the men who would be returning: Dennis, Don, Ron, and Ed. "We should have another good crew this year," he wrote, "with all of you to help train the new men. Everyone is predicting a hot, dry summer this year. If so we should have a pretty busy season."

The letter, which I didn't see until long after my brother was gone, closes with "about your brother and his friend, I can't promise anything, but I will sure keep them in mind. It is always possible that someone won't show up, and we would need a replacement or two. From what you have told me about them, they both sound like real good fellows to have." I have no idea who my friend was, and I had not known my brother tried to get me in.

By mid-June, my brother would be gone to the mountains. I remember him describing nights in the bunkhouse, high on the mountain, as the men listened to dry lightning and rolling thunder dance across the peaks. They would be chanting, "Strike! Strike!" So hungry were they for the adrenalin rush of camaraderie fighting a runaway firestorm.

Off hours, they would take turns diving for cans of beer dropped into a freezing mountain pool under the waterfall. Or there was the contest: could you eat a whole peeled orange without laughing or choking to death? I remember my brother giving me a demonstration, jamming the orange in his mouth, the juice running down his chin and soaking his shirt as he chomped and chortled the orange, gnashing it down with hilarity.

On this boisterous, heroic crew of manly men, they called my brother Twiggy, after the mod waif of London fashion. Smallest in the crew, he came last in line when they savaged a path through the forest ahead of the fire. Others might wield a bulldozer, chainsaw, gas-powered brush-cutter, ax, or a Pulaski. Then came Twiggy with his rake to claw off duff and leave bare mineral soil in the fire's path. Far from the easiest job, some days this was the hardest—skipping about just ahead of the flames, all the work of the others depending on my brother's ballet with his rake to keep a swirl of sparks from jumping the line.

One time they got surrounded, the crew boss shouting, "Run!" And they all dropped their tools and sprinted through a descending cloud of sparks and ash. Behind them, they could hear the fire seize the truck with a tremendous boom. As my brother told me later, at times like these the taste of terror and thrill combined, as you ran with your crew through blue trees quivering in the path of fire.

Another time, the fire mostly subdued, they were caught by darkness, and bedded down for the night around a big old snag. They knew the fire had gotten into the trunk, and smoldered there. Too tired to care. But sometime after midnight, a shout, "She's coming down." And they all stared upward, trying to get a fix on the snag against the stars as it tilted, leaned, fell, and exploded on impact, burst into flames, somehow missing everyone.

I have the photograph I took of that stalwart crew in their hickory shirts, stagged pants, suspenders, and brash grins. They were a company of joyful renegades, and my brother was one of the men.

## FOLDING THE TENT

My brother and Lynne had decided to marry. They had camped in the backyard at our parents' house for a visit, then were packing to head north to Nanaimo for the wedding. We would follow a few days later. I was away somewhere, and it was our mother who overheard Bret talking with Lynne in the yard as they rolled up the tent and tried to stow it in its stuff sack.

"I won't have Kim to show me how to do this kind of thing," he said.

Can this story be true? I have heard our mother tell it several times. The implication is that Bret was limited in camping skills and confessed this to his wife. But the Bret I knew was at least my equal in this manly art, and probably my superior. The story has long troubled me.

## "YOU CAN'T EAT BEAUTY"

Bret got married, got his degree, returned to Oregon and completed a second master's degree at Oregon State University, this time in geography and planning. Then he took a job in Hood River, an hour east of Portland, with the Planning Department there. Despite his study of history, anthropology, and geography, he had to make his living enforcing the regulations.

One day, he was with a group of Hood River County movers and shakers—a county commissioner, the mayor, a local developer, various other worthies. They were standing on a bluff late in the day looking down on an island of a few acres in the Columbia River. The task was to decide what to "do" with the island. As my brother told me the story later, the conversation went like this.

"We could carve out a little marina at this end," said the developer, "put in some nice homes. Very high end. Think of the tax revenues, gentlemen. Good for my company, good for the county."

"What we really need, though," said the commissioner, "is gravel. Water-level access to quality fill—that's gold these days. We could crush it here, or do the rough break on site, and barge the boulders for further crushing at a facility downstream. Leave a nice deep channel where that island used to be."

There was a beat of silence as they all indulged in imagining the island gone.

"It's beautiful," my brother said. The sun had dipped low, and gold light flickered in the willows that fringed the shore. A kingfisher called. A breeze traced a ripple across flat water, limpid in the sun.

"You can't eat beauty, Bret," said the commissioner. "That's all nice. I like it as well as the next guy. But you can't eat beauty."

Later, when my brother was working in Salem, sometimes I would visit him in his corner of the county office building. His love of Oregon, of the land, of the wild had led him to get an MA in geography, but he had become a planner, a practical prophet. His desk was in good order, but clearly overwhelmed by paper, files, maps. His job was to tell people what they could or could not do. It was a warm day, and as he swiveled slightly in his chair, I could sense our moment was an unusual pause in a life of frenzy.

"People cry all the time," he said. "They come to ask why they can't do what they've always wanted to do, why some statute has to apply to them. I tell them the laws have to apply to everyone, and then they cry—or swear. Sometimes they swear at me." There was a hum in the office all around us, a resonance that spoke of order and the law, good intentions and heartless restraint.

"When I worked in Hood River," he said, "there was a typo on the door to my office. It said 'Offical Room' instead of 'Official.' The staff kept saying they were going to change it, but that never happened. And eventually, it did seem like the Offical Room. The laws were based on good intentions, but in practice they could seem fickle, arbitrary. Sometimes, when people came in to complain, I had to explain regulations in great detail that I did not quite believe." He paused, and his gray eyes looked at me. "I have become they," he said, "as in 'They won't let you do what you have always wanted with your own land.' People hate me."

# BOOK IV. SEE YOU TOMORROW

# PATH TO THE SUN

My brother was dead, gone—and I was alone. I was cut off from my own story as I had known it by the bullet that took him. The path that I had seen before me for my life was pulled away. From that last day of his life, I stumbled into the first of mine, the new, ragged era with no rules, no assurance. I would have to build this life from scratch. It wasn't a matter of getting over his death. His death was a single moment for him, but an endless, unforgiving moment for me, for us, for every encounter from then forward with others—and every encounter with myself. I had come to the crevasse and could not cross. I would have to circle back, far back, start a new journey. I would have to explore old terrain in a new light. His suicide was my book of genesis: and darkness was on the face of the waters—stubborn darkness that no hand could brush aside.

The day my brother took his life, as evening came we were gathered at my sister Barb's house in Portland, and my sisters and I decided to sleep on the floor. Three in a row. Our brother was gone. How could we deserve a bed, comfort, rest?

As I closed my eyes, in my mind I abruptly saw my brother on a path in the mountains. He was beyond me, above me, where the trail led through the trees toward the ridge.

His steps slowed, and he turned to face me. Without a word his gaze begged me to call him back. His eyes, hurt and pleading, wanted me to reach with my soul to gather him back to life. But in this trance, with my eyes, I willed him to go on.

With one last look over his shoulder, he turned from me, and started up the path toward the ridgeline. He reached the summit, and disappeared into the rising sun.

When I looked down to the path at my feet, it was pulled away like a rope. I was alone in the forest.

## HALF A GOOD THING

A week later, I was scheduled to give a lecture on the poetry of Sylvia Plath. I called the program organizers and said I could not do this. Plath's suicide, my brother's—there was no way I could witness in a public setting about such things.

The reply was that the show must go on. Fine, I thought. What do I have to lose beyond everything I have lost?

The event was in the sanctuary of the Unitarian Church in downtown Portland. Maybe a hundred people filed into the pews. I showed the film on Plath. When the story came to Plath's last day, Plath sealing the door to the nursery with tape, then turning on the gas at the stove—I felt my breath grow short. I saw my brother's face, pleading with me. I felt his ribs, when he sobbed in my arms. I saw our father, unable to sit with us at the memorial service, so broken he was—haunting the back of the room, then gone.

The lights came up, and I made my way to the podium. I held a kind of script about Plath's career as a poet, a selection of her poems to read, questions to pose, notes for discussion. Can I remember what I said? It was impossible. But here are the words my tunnel of memory delivers from that night.

"Thank you for coming this evening. I hope you have enjoyed the film. . . ." My heart was pounding. Silence killed my brother. Not telling killed him. Go deeper.

"I have to say," I may have said, "that in my view Sylvia Plath did half a good thing for us. She told difficult things, she witnessed great darkness, passion, anger, and she left searing poems that startled us. Then she took her life. She did not do the whole story of a life, but she did the dark part very well.

"I have to tell you that last week my brother took his life." For a moment I could not speak another word. I felt I was back in the realm of my vision, that my eyes, pleading with others in the room, would have to do the work between us, for no words would come. No words would do. We were suspended in a silence, like suffocation, like a prayer of fury, like the moment when my brother could not decide what to do, just before the end. I took a long, slow breath.

"Let me read Sylvia Plath's poem 'Daddy.' And I invite you to think of someone in your life who has called up your anger, your resentment. Maybe there are three stages in such a relation: silence, angry words, and somewhere beyond that anger, a struggle toward reconciliation. Let's hear her poem." But then I knew my limits. "Could someone read 'Daddy'?"

## WHITE ALICE

I had a job in Alaska. It made no sense to go. But nothing made sense. There was a ticket, a flight, and by evening after a full day of travel I was bedding down in a quad of the empty student dormitory of Kuskokwim Community College, at the edge of Bethel, far out on the tundra.

Late, but darkness would not come. I should have been planning the faculty workshop I was to conduct the next day, but that felt pointless. I had to walk, out from my room, from the building, and west along the road that rose and fell as the earth buckled over permafrost in the short summer season.

I passed the health center, an industrial shop, and the last scattered houses with their barking dogs, as the road led on. The sun was gone below the horizon, but the air glowed over the open land. No trees, low hills, blue distances. And off across the tundra, the tower they called White Alice, once part of the Distant Early Warning line in case of Soviet attack. In those days, our bombers had been in the air around the clock, airborne in case the command came to fly their mission of doom west across Siberia toward the people we had learned to fear and hate. White Alice, now a rusted tower, sent guidance to pilots in their long dream of vigilance, droning over the earth with A-bomb trigger ready.

Away from the road, I lay down on the reindeer moss and looked up at the first stars. And suddenly it came to me: How much warning did my brother give? Years! Years of pain, sagas of silence, looks of yearning, cryptic hints that I, a damn fool for all my training in nuance in a poem's lyric, could not catch.

Shouldn't I remain on this bed ground for good? What sense did it make to be a teacher? Fool. Blind fool. Cruel brother. Shouldn't I strike out beyond the last of Bethel's roads and seek my brother somewhere far across the open land?

I remembered a night late in my marriage. At a conference on Shakespeare on Halloween night at Sunriver, a resort south of Bend, I had felt I did not belong there, or anywhere. So despite the late hour, I started driving. Home? Maybe. Somewhere. The moon was full, and I let the car find its own direction, north to Bend, west through Sisters, and up over the hump of the Cascade Mountains.

A little after midnight, the car turned off at a place called Lost Lake, at the foot of the jagged peak called Three-Fingered Jack. It was a barren place at that season, and very cold. The car stopped in the empty campground, around the shore of the lake from the highway. I left the car and stood in the moonlight at the water's edge. What was my plan? Gradually, I realized my plan was to be cold. To see how cold I could get. A chill wind swept across the water to me. Now and then, a long-haul truck's beam of light would swivel across the water and disappear toward the west, or toward the east, leaving me in the moonwash. My plan would work. Cold fingered through my thin clothes, and began to crawl into my heart. This was fitting, right.

The question I carry from that night: what calibration in my makeup caused me to turn, at just the moment I still could—turn and stumble to the car, just before my cold-stiffened hands could not open the door, fumble the key into the ignition, and drive west toward my life? That little turn, that tiny adjustment at the boundary—what turned me back where my brother went on?

## PARIS RAIN

There were so many things I never asked my brother. That summer of 1969, when we had planned to meet in Paris, but in the end I had taken another road—what did he do in that city, as it dawned on him I would not appear? I never asked, will never know.

After a time, I had to go to Paris to be alone. My marriage had ended, and my brother had died. I needed to get outside all that and see where I might turn. This was my part of survival: not to buck up, not to break down I needed to ride the waves of sorrow and the strange exhilaration that sorrow can offer, out of its back pocket, when you realize you have, against great odds, continued to breathe, to use words, to dream, and that you are lucky to see the sun come up at dawn.

In Paris, there is a clown named Buffo. By day, this man works with autistic children. By night, he is Buffo the autistic clown, hesitant, motionless, helpless, silent, ready to explode with love, hate, brilliance, despair.

I have seen him on stage barely moving for twenty minutes, and everyone spellbound. The slightest twitch or glance shouts his longing and his pain.

Buffo has a custom with his apartment: when an artist arrives in Paris, an artist in need of silence, he leaves the key with his concierge and moves to his girlfriend's place. So I was at Buffo's flat on Rue de la Folie-Méricourt, climbing the seventh turning of the stair, turning the old key at the door for the garret of two rooms, with pigeons chanting, and the rain drumming the tiles outside the window. I would put on my coat and hat, and walk Rue du Chemin Vert to Boulevard Beaumarchais, past the Place des Vosges to Rue Vieille du Temple, and then down along Rue du Pont Louis-Philippe to the Seine, to the downstream tip of the Île de la Cité to sit at the Pointe du Vert

Galant, under the willow, and watch the river, divided by the islands, come back together into one. I stared and stared at the way the water curled there, as it joined again, as it healed.

One night, I went to watch a train depart at the Gare d'Austerlitz. A friend was to take that train to Barcelona. She had agreed to meet with me before departure, to help me. Not lover. Friend. But she did not appear—at eight . . . at nine . . . at eleven. I never did learn what happened, why she did not show herself.

At the bitter end of my rope, I watched the train pull out at midnight, watched the red lantern on the last car dwindle, the red light taper, the life principle wither, my brother's heart contract, my brother's friendship go.

As I walked in the rain back toward Buffo's street, I realized I was feverish. Hot, chilled, clamped with sweat, shaken. My hand on the walls of buildings I passed, to steady myself. Over the Pont Neuf, then the zigzag dizzy stagger up into my neighborhood, fumbling for the code at the street door, staggering up the seven turnings of the stair. Inside Buffo's room, I slumped to the floor, lay flat on my back, and closed my eyes. I was falling down a shaft, a tunnel, a cavern. The air grew darker, denser, my breath grew thick. But at the bottom, there was no impact, only a burst of light, and in that light a voice: "No woman will save you from the destiny, the difficulty, of being who you are."

## TALKING RECKLESSLY

When we were young, our father had a habit of abruptly increasing the voltage by announcing, "Let's talk recklessly!" This meant any tiptoeing in polite banter was over. We were to dig deep, gossip freely about our uncertainties and strange beliefs, lean forward and tumble into the liveliest possible interchange.

This verve matched his habit as a writer to speak boldly beyond fear, reticence, or even the need to be strong or eloquent. "I must be willingly fallible," he said once, "in order to deserve a place in the realm where miracles happen." And part of such necessary fallibility required trying out wild things in language, and speaking with zest.

When I think of our father's way with a conversation, I see it as vertical—always going deeper. At his best, he wanted to know what was at the foundation, hidden, waiting. A different way of talk can be horizontal—you move from one topic to the next, skimming cream as you find it. But for our father, the gold lay deep, and he was ready to plunge.

I think he got this habit from his mother. My aunt Mar says that when she was being courted by our father's brother Bob, back in Hutchinson, Kansas, in the 1930s, "It was a thrill to be at the Stafford house, because they talked about all kinds of things in all kinds of ways. You didn't go there to hide and listen. You went there to talk, and laugh, and learn."

This does not mean irresponsible ventures. Quite the opposite. At best, talking recklessly means deeply responsible ventures of creative inquiry unencumbered by rules of polite restraint. Our father was a citizen writer—involved in all kinds of creative activity—and his legacy called for broad citizen involvement, not just literary creations. As the writer Elizabeth Woody says, "Responsibility means responding to your abilities."

The mystery is that for all his advocacy of freedom in writing and his zest for exploratory talk at home, about certain things with our father you couldn't get a word. He never talked with me about my brother's death. Something stopped him. Was this reticence the code of survival that helped him, as it helped his generation, to make it through the Great Depression—and in his own case, through World War II and beyond as a pacifist, an edge-dweller in a time of symphonic military patriotism?

Our father ends his poem "Vocation" with a father saying to a son: "Your job is to find what the world is trying to be." Somehow, in that quest, he could not speak with us about the puzzle of his own dead son, his fears, the dense interior of his pain. Or as he says in his one poem about my brother, "Why tell what hurts?"

It wasn't until I read his journal, for example, that I learned the act of teaching could be as frightening to my father as it sometimes was for me.

I thought he was the master, never at a loss. It was I who fretted anxiously before a class, and might spend much of the following night awake, going over what I had not done right. But there it is in his journal, after he had been teaching college for over ten years: "Back to school today. When I stood—1st hour—and first looked at the students, I thought I'd throw up. But all students were nice today." I would have been helped by knowing my fears were not an aberration, an idiosyncratic failure. And I suspect this knowledge might have helped my brother, too.

This is the silence in my father's practice, and my family's culture, when things get hard. This is the gap that I must close for my own life. For there is so much I don't know. I have not read my brother's journal, if he kept one. I have not talked with his wife in over twenty years. I have lived essentially in silence in my own family about my brother. I do not know—beyond his one poem on the subject—our father's thoughts. I have never heard a detailed account of finding Bret dead from my sister. So what do I know? I have to make the most of the materials that are available to me—memory, dreams, a handful of artifacts, photographs, and archaeology of soul.

In the years since my brother died, and then my father, this archaeology digs deeper. Once at a gathering, my poetry teacher from college took me aside and said, "There is something I have thought about telling you for a long time, but kept to myself. It's about your father. Should I tell you?"

"Fire away," I said.

"Well, you see, your father and I were driving home from a conference late one night, many years ago. We got to talking about our children. And eventually Bill said a strange thing. 'I love all my children,' he said, 'but there is one who is myself—and that's Kim.'"

I felt a knife pierce my heart. For a moment, I could not speak.

"I can see why you hesitated," I said. "That's heavy."

"I couldn't carry it any more. Do with it what you will."

In the years since that conversation, I have thought often of this pronouncement by our father, in secret, to a friend, for hiding. Realistically, can such a thing be hidden? No, it can't. My brother grew up in a house where he was not the son presumed by our father to inherit the kingdom.

Being orphaned from this inheritance was not for lack of trying by the oldest boy. When I look back now, I see that my brother worked hard in myriad dimensions to follow the father we all admired. It was my brother who made little books as a child. It was my brother who pioneered pacifism in our father's footsteps, who worked for the Forest Service as our father had done, who tried teaching at a series of community colleges. These parts of the quest he could accomplish. The difficult dimension, though, was how Bret strove to re-create his apprehension of our father's ethical stance. That was hardest. Bret caught the moral standard, in spades, but not enough seasoning of forgiveness for imperfection.

Our father clearly loved my brother, admired him, viewed him as a standard of behavior for the rest of us. But my brother was not our father. Identity was withheld from him—in my view, at great cost to both of them.

The remedy for hard silences about crucial matters seems so simple: When you are together, in one place, be together truly. Tell your troubles, your confusions. Without answers, you can still be together in the search. You must be reckless.

The thirteenth-century Persian poet Rumi pointed out a simple fact about human behavior: it's a good conversation, he said, when two people can talk about the same thing. In my life, I observe—in both myself and others—a different habit: we talk about different things at the same time. This is marked by the relative rarity of the following sentence in the flow of our conversations: "Tell me more." When I remember life with my brother, always eager to tell him what I was accomplishing, I said this too rarely.

Our father used to give a writing assignment to his students: "Think of something you did, but write about what you might have done. Or think about something you said, but write about what you might have said." His idea was that a writer could have a second chance to get things right. There was a kind of alchemy available in language to turn regret into creation.

Some time after my brother's death, his wife came to visit our parents. I was away. And when I returned, as often, I was so busy catching up with my work, my self-designed life of frenzy, I did not learn about that visit in detail. But now I have a copy of my father's letter to Lynne after she had departed for her home in Canada. The letter is an unusual document, for the great poet, the man of words who trumpeted the habit of "talking recklessly" in pursuit of discovery, confesses his reticence, and laments what he could not say or do. He says to Lynne:

> When you cried, getting out of the car on arrival, I should have known that maybe we could find our voices and bring into speech many recollections, thoughts about what might have been, ideas about going on into the future with some soothing realizations and helpful conclusions. But I let my timidity keep me from exploring how to talk about the past and think about the future. I wanted you to feel right. I wanted to help. But I didn't know how. I felt like a mirror being carried through a crowd, not knowing what to reflect.

This reticence of my father, my own reticence on many occasions, the reticence of my whole family since my brother's death—this is a contradiction to the long-cherished notion of "talking recklessly" that governed much of our history. It was as if Lynne, simply by crying openly, said more than any of us could say.

## KULEANA

After my brother died, I would talk about him very early in a conversation with anyone I met. I remember awkward dates, where my abrupt mention of my brother's suicide stopped the conversation cold. One poor woman wept. Our coffee grew cold, and the date was at an end. It was as if I could not proceed on any basis except full disclosure, as I saw it, feeling a clumsy loyalty to my brother's sorrow beyond care for the person across the table from me.

What shall I do with this awkward habit?

Sometimes in writing class I give the prompt to my students, "What was your job as a child?"

"Our jobs?" they say.

"You know, the task you figured out you had to do in the family drama."

Ah, yes . . . We all begin to write, and after a time, when we share, students shock me with their early vocations:

"My job was to be good so our father wouldn't leave."

"I was the nice girl so my mom wouldn't feel like a failure."

"I took care of my baby brother because he seemed to be invisible to everyone else."

I think my brother, as I have said, saw his job as becoming the ethical heir to our parents and the model child. My job was to watch him and learn. And my job now is to be the one who asks questions, who blunders into tough talk, who tries to seek with stories.

There is a word in the Hawaiian language I have come to trust: *kuleana*. *Kuleana* means the freedom to tell one's own stories, to offer what has come to you freely and with confidence. Certain stories have been given to you along your life path—by others, by experience, by hardship, by living in a place—and you are allowed to tell them. But *kuleana* also carries the meaning of responsibility: Which stories must you never tell? And for the stories you will tell, how will you tell them? What is the right time, and the right way to tell particular stories—to family, to a friend, to a stranger? What stories are right for a child? What story would you tell to someone you will not see again, by way of brave affection and farewell? What is the story, what is the time, what is the way of unfolding? Each story will seek the right listener in the right way because you live by *kuleana*.

And to whom must you tell the hardest stories, the ones that require brave listening? For me, these are the Bret stories I must tell here. For this is not a book about suicide or, finally, about my brother. It is a book about the tricks required to become a human being, in my case a man, as I have begun to learn these tricks from my brother's life, our father's life, my son's life, and my own.

As the writer Stephen Dunn has said, we long to convert the simple events of our lives into legend. Or as the writer Dian Million says, stories are our oldest way to stop time. It is in this spirit that I keep remembering my brother, am caught and held by his stories, and in this way, as the only way I have, I continue to live in his story by *Kuleana.*

## RÉSUMÉ OF FAILURES

When I was young, hunched beside my brother on a threadbare couch in southwest Portland, as I have said, our mother or father would read from the book *Fifty Famous Stories.* This little bible held parables of how, when one is cast down, great learning comes. Remember with me, for example, the story of Alfred and the Oat Cakes:

King Alfred has failed. He can't unite his country. Norse invaders rule. Alfred's army is scattered, and Alfred is alone, in rags, stumbling from place to place. He comes to a hut and asks for food. No one knows he is king, and he is too ashamed to tell.

"Old man, if you will watch these oat cakes by the fire," says the woman of the house, "I will give you one." So Alfred settles down by the fire to watch. In flickering flames, he sees his kingdom's dissolution. All old glory crumbles from the embers.

But as he continues to stare, in the flames he begins to see one thing he might do to gather his people. Then another. Gradually, a detailed plan forms in his mind.

"Fool!" shouts the old woman. "The oat cakes are burned, and you shall have none."

Beside my brother, listening to our mother read, I was changed by this story, and by many like it. A seed was planted in my mind: Success does not kindle success. Happiness is born in struggle and even in failure.

This idea lay dormant for decades. I began to advance in the public realm, spending twelve years at the University of Oregon, getting a PhD, finding jobs here and there, beginning to publish a few things. Every time I revised my résumé, there was more stuff—jobs, publications, "distinctions." I wrote a book called *Having Everything Right*, the title based on the Kwakiutl name *helade* for a place on Vancouver Island—a place of great abundance and good life. After the book came out, my friends teased me: "So, Mr. Having Everything Right, how goes the perfect life?"

The perfect life? Well, mine did not match the résumé. My life, in fact, was composed largely of errors, losses, times of disorientation, and failure. As a friend said to me once, there is a great difference between trying to be humble, and being humbled. Life has humbled me.

Years later, after our father had died, I was writing a book about his life, and my life with him. I sent a few chapters to an old friend of our father's, Robert Bly. Expecting a detailed analysis of my writing, I was surprised when the response came as a postcard: "You are more interesting when you talk about your failures." Well, I thought, if that is the case, then I am lucky: I have an abundance of those.

A short time later, in writing class, one of my students made a startling suggestion. We had been sifting our memories for stories, writing in response to a series of prompts I had offered, but we weren't making much progress. "Could we write a résumé of our failures?" he said.

"How would that work?"

"Well, you know, when you write a résumé, you list the so-called 'high points'—education, awards, jobs, all the big-deal stuff. But if your life is like mine, you had to pay for those with a string of disasters. It seems like we might find something to write about there."

So we tried: list your accomplishments . . . and then, for each, tell what really happened "behind the scenes." My own take:

PhD in Medieval Literature . . .

*What was I thinking, to squander my twenties on scholarship, a practice with puzzling short-take rewards but ultimately toxic to my soul? I was a wanderer, a poet, lost romantic. Yet I pored over criticism, labored at Latin, typed a 300-page dissertation my advisor called "possibly the most turgid prose ever penned." I was so lonely, I would go down by the river before dawn, feel the cold seep into my body, and watch the purling current carry my hopes away.*

Founding Director, Northwest Writing Institute . . .

*The disproportion between the magnitude of the name and the size of the operation was extreme. "Northwest?" I was a one-person insomniac worrying through programs I could not do well, without an office at the college, carrying my files in a wooden box slung over my shoulder that my friends called "Kim's shoe-shine kit."*

Governor's Arts Award for service to the literary community of Oregon . . .

*I can't govern my own life, which has become a frenetic series of engagements lurching along on too little sleep, and enabled by frequent neglect of my family, my health, and my own creative life.*

Taught at Lewis & Clark College for thirty years . . .

*Hunkered down at the school where my father taught, surely holding the record for the number of successive one-year contracts, I have what I call "self-conferred tenure"—meaning I am not capable of departure.*

Author of *The Muses Among Us: Eloquent Listening and Other Pleasures of the Writer's Craft* . . .

*I was so wrapped up in service to others, I let my brother die. He was in obvious pain, faltering, in despair. Eloquent listening? I did not hear him, even as I preached the gospel of eloquent listening to students in class after class. . . .*

As I compose this sequence, I recognize a perverse code in professional life: each named accomplishment may hide the true life of struggle, faltering, failure. I have been forced to acknowledge over time that, in my life, I am something of an expert in this area.

On my daily walks before dawn along the steep downhill road through the cemetery near my house, I often have thoughts "out of nowhere." Recently, as the stars glittered high and an owl called from the ravine to my right, I became aware of a sentence in my mind: "I need to forgive myself." I carried a heaviness, a dull ache that resolved itself into these words. But forgive myself for what? As I walked on, a second owl called from the forest to my left, and the answer came into my mind: "I need to forgive myself for being Kim."

What can that mean? Forgive myself? As I pondered, I realized my psyche works like this: When I do something that does not pan out, that is something wrong, and something wrong is something bad, and when I do something bad, I am a bad person. As if by psychic voodoo, if someone near me gives me the silent treatment, I default to the explanation that they think I am bad, and so I am.

I'm not proud of this habit in my mind. In fact, it drives me crazy, shuts me down, makes me mute. I perpetuate the problem by the habits I learned young. The operating system for assessing self-worth by the silence of another is clearly prone to error, and can cause great damage. But there it is.

As I stumbled along in the dark between the stones that marked the end of life after life, I became aware that some variation of this psychic logic, flaws and all, took my brother down. He lost job, house, happiness . . . and then he went into personal darkness, stopped sleeping, became immune to consolation, and took his life.

The writer James Hillman identifies "story consciousness" as the essential skill for psychic survival. If you are raised on stories, he says, you recognize that the life path goes spiraling down for a time, faltering, failing . . . but then there is a turning, and things get better—things trend upward for a time, and you prevail, gather momentum, succeed . . . and then there is a another turning, and your personal hero's journey falters again. Plotted on the wall, this undulating path that rises, falls, and rises again can form a classic wave pattern—crest, and trough, and crest.

As I have pondered this pattern, I have begun to recognize a stern outcome in my brother's life. If you do not have story consciousness, and you are on the way up, when the turning comes you may think this is the end of your story: you are a failure, period. Or when you are on your way down, you may think, again, that failure is your whole story. In either case, not to expect the turning can spell your doom.

Thinking like this killed my brother. Traveling down toward darkness, he thought this trajectory final, inescapable, the true and final story of his life. He saw the trend but not the pattern.

When I began to write this book, I Googled "Bret Stafford." Since he died before the rise of the Internet, entries are few. I find his master's thesis about harmonious relations. And I find his name listed at a site called "400 Historic Suicides." Along with Samson, Socrates, Judas, Sylvia Plath, and Kurt Cobain, I find my brother:

+ bret stafford (william's son, kim's brother) – 1988

A note at the head of the list indicates the plus sign means "inspirational (influenced illustrious work)." I presume this refers to our father's poem about my brother, but how strange. If the implied trade is a life for a poem, we really burned the oat cake there.

How many oat cakes have I burned? Trading freedom in my twenties for a PhD. Trading time with my family for the governor's approval. Of course, it's all complicated. But today, as I write, I have turned sixty-two, and it is necessary to take a hard look at what I choose to do with the balance of this life.

I have learned success means surviving a significant failure, with learning. Failure means an episode of success without some hard-won wisdom for the lean times that are sure to come.

# THE NEXT LIFE

Our son, Guthrie, told me once that he sees most adults "just running toward the next life . . . and as they get older, they run faster." My brother started the next life at forty, when he departed from this world. And I believe his death began the next life for me, in this world. I live now in a realm where everything has changed, and the old ways of hiding begin to fall away.

When I was a child, my grandmother gave me a book called *Ishi in Two Worlds*, about the "last wild Indian" of California who stumbled into the twentieth century in 1911, alone, and starving. He was the lone survivor of the Yahi people, and he was following the Feather River south to find that place in the Yahi creation story where people who have died go through a tunnel into the next world. This story itself was a kind of creation myth for my own childhood, and I spent many days imagining that I, too, was the last of my kind.

There is one incident in Ishi's life that teaches me about my brother. In the summer of 1915, the anthropologists took Ishi back to his native ground, on Deer Creek, in northern California. Ishi was very uneasy about the journey. He recognized the local guide, a man named Apperson, as someone who had harried his people toward the end. One night by the fire in camp, as Apperson was cleaning his gun, Ishi asked quietly, "Are you going to shoot me now?" He was in the terrain where he and his people had been hunted to extinction.

As the party went deeper into the canyon, Ishi became more wary. Finally, one night he left the camp in the dark. Again, he was alone in the place of ghosts, as he had been in the years after the last of his people were gone.

When he returned to camp in the morning, he told the young boy in the party, Saxton Pope Jr., that in the dark he had learned that his people were all right. They had made it to the next world, he said, and all was well. For the balance of the expedition, Ishi was in good spirits, showing the anthropologists how he speared salmon in the creek, made a bow and arrows, hunted and dressed a deer, made fire, named his people's places of hunting and hiding, and identified a hundred plants that had kept his people alive.

I think the comfort in that return to camp for Ishi combined a sense that his people were well, and also that the next world, when his own time came, would be ready to welcome him.

Shortly after my brother died, when I was in the darkest passage of my own survival, I had a letter from Naomi, an old friend in Texas, telling me that my brother had appeared to her in a dream and said to her: "Tell Kim I am okay. Will you let him know? I am doing what I need to do, and I am well."

Where is he, then? When he went through that primordial tunnel at death, where did he come forth?

I believe this life had become a tunnel of suffering for my brother, with deep depression, and the only way he could come forth was through death. When Bret wrote his senior thesis in anthropology at the University of Oregon, in 1970, his scholarship became a parable for his life of struggle. His *Understanding Maori Taboo* begins with a kind of genesis statement about a world filled with danger. When I read his words now, his voice sounds distanced from the spirit of those times, the 1960s, that famous era of free love:

> All men, upon birth, enter a world which is not of their own making. It is a world which existed before man and which constantly eludes his efforts to comprehend and control it. It can hardly be said, from man's perspective, to be the epitome of order. . . .
>
> But men seem to need order, to need a system of some kind, that they may feel secure. They cannot live with disorder. Thus, they build a system; they *impose* order upon the world. The source of the system of order they adopt is their culture. . . .
>
> But the world is not completely amenable to the system of order men have imposed upon it. Plus, it is full of dangers. . . . And it is here that taboo comes in.

Taboo, "a ritual restriction or prohibition," became my brother's code.

It has taken me over twenty years to realize my brother came to a point where he could not live. He loved his family, and his life had many blessings. But he had to stop his pain and did not have the skills to come to safety in some other way. I could run from my life—by divorce, by wandering, by writing a fierce new self-definition. My brother did not have these devious means.

Once, when weeping took me down, I could hardly breathe, thinking of him. "Why did you have to go?" This chain of words were like mountains that could not be moved, a wall blocking my path: Why-Did-You-Have-to-Go? But as I gasped, the mountain words were jolted to a new configuration in my mind, and I could breathe again: You-Have-Gone. The question that had choked me became a fact. My brother has gone.

Recently I found a long letter he wrote from Iowa—not to the family, as was his custom, but to me. It was November of 1966, and winter was closing down over the Grinnell campus. He had just been telling me about his efforts to be a good person, not selfish, or jealous. "I, as I think all of us do," he wrote, "have a slight tendency to think a lot of myself. I try to get away from this." But then he lets himself go, revealing in words the heart of his desire:

> Way back in August, as the jet took off, I craned over (probably irritating the fellow next to me) to take a look at the Cascade range. Boy did it look good! I could see the mountains way up in Washington, and clear down, I think, to the Diamond Peak area. But the best part was looking down on Jefferson Park. I could see the ridge and the hidden, far-away valley. I wished I had a parachute.

## "WHAT DO YOU WANT?"

The summer after my brother's death, I was teaching a week-long writing class on the Oregon coast. My divorce had been finalized in June, I was living in the house on Custer Street where Bret had last visited me, and I was bouncing along from one short teaching stint to the next. But I wasn't teaching writing any more. That did not make sense. Instead, I was reaching for the deepest stories people had to offer. "What have you been carrying?" I began to say. "What secret are you ready to tell?" I could not teach a class, or have a conversation, without mentioning my brother, his pain, his suicide. I felt like the dancer with the red shoes, unable to stop public performances of pain.

In this class, one student in particular seemed alive to the darkness I was swimming through. She asked about my brother after class one day and seemed ready to listen to anything I had to say.

On Friday afternoon, the last day, everyone shared something they had written, we savored what we had managed to bring to light, and then the writers got up to leave.

But this one lingered. When the others had left the room, she said to me, "Well, Kim Stafford, let's go on an adventure."

"Umm, like what?" I said.

"Oh . . . let's go camping. Would you like that?"

"Okay," I said. "Where? When?"

"Pick me up a week from today," she said, "say 3 p.m., and we'll decide about the where." She put her hand on my shoulder. "And in the meantime," she said, "be good to yourself." Then she gave me her address, took up her notebook, and was gone.

Earlier that summer, I had gone to buy myself a new sleeping bag at REI. The clerk was an old friend, Gil, a crag rat from way back.

"You just became single," he said, "didn't you?"

"Yes."

"Well you don't need a sleeping bag, then. You need two sleeping bags that zip together."

"I do?"

"Trust me."

The following Friday, I packed the two sleeping bags, my tent and stove, gathered food, took a map of the Mount Jefferson Wilderness, locked my house, and went to get her. She came skipping out of her apartment downtown with her backpack over her shoulder and climbed into the car, and we were off.

"East slope of Mount Jefferson okay with you?" I said, as we eased onto the freeway, heading south.

"Whatever you say," she said. "Haven't been there, and that's always good. By the way, my boyfriend is really pissed about this."

"Your boyfriend? I didn't know you had a boyfriend."

"Yeah, he says how come you're going hiking with this other guy, and you won't go with me?"

"What did you tell him?"

"I told him if I wuss out on the trail, he would make me feel bad about it. But you won't."

"Why would I?" I said.

"Exactly."

At that moment, as we were climbing the grade out of town on I-5 South, I noticed a silver band on her ring finger.

"Say," I said, "can you tell me about that ring? I hadn't noticed it before."

"That's my promise to myself never to marry," she said. We drove in silence for a time. I tried to make all this fit together—an adventure . . . a boyfriend . . . a vow.

By six, we were on the trail at Candle Creek, heading west toward Mount Jefferson through open stands of Douglas fir and ponderosa pine. Huckleberries were ripening, and we stopped now and then to gather a handful, readjust our packs, and cut a couple of walking sticks from an alder stand at the periphery of the lava flow that paralleled the trail.

It was dusk by the time we left the trail and scrambled half a mile cross-country to a lake without a name, a blue dot on my map. We set up the tent. Clouds were gathering.

I held up the two sleeping bags I had taken from my pack. "Shall I zip these together?"

"I don't plan on being cold," she said. "Do you?"

So we had a quick dinner and climbed into the bag together. I had fit a candle stub to the toe of my boot with hot wax, and light flickered on the walls of the tent.

"I'm here to talk," she said. "How about you?"

So that's what we did, all that night and into the next day. She told me about her family, her journey from Idaho to Oregon, teaching unwed mothers, alternative education, dark family stories and scenes of illumination through friendship and self-discovery. I told her about my family, my brother's childhood, making my living as a scholar gypsy, being a teacher all over. I told her how my father's advice for writers seemed useful for my life: when it gets hard, lower your standards and keep going.

At one point, just before dawn, she said, "We've talked about your daughter, about writing, about our families, war, fear, hurt and sorrow—now let's do God." So we did God for awhile. She had been on the "God Squad" in college, and I, with my brother, co-moderator of the Presbyterian Youth. And then it was noon.

We packed the tent, the sleeping bags, what was left of our food, and started down the trail, walking much of the way in silence, stopping now and then to rest, and tasting again of the huckleberry. She took the lead, and I followed. No other hiker on that trail the whole six miles.

When we were maybe a mile from the road, she turned around, planted her walking stick, turned her head to the side, and said, "Well, Kim Stafford, what do you want?" In the momentum of our long conversation, I thought I had the answer.

"I want to be a good father," I said, "to my daughter, Rosie."

"We talked about family last night," she said. "But now we're talking about you. What do you want?" She was looking at me with a smile. She had all the time in the world.

"Well," I said, "I want to be a good writer, then. After Rosie, that's the most important thing."

"You're not hearing me," she said. "We talked about writing last night, along with everything else. But I'm asking now about you. What do YOU want?"

"People are always asking me that," I said. "And I don't know."

"You need to know," she said. "I'm in no hurry." She leaned back, but did not set her pack on the ground, and neither did I. It was not time to rest.

I realized, as she waited, that all my life I had set this question aside. In my family, the training was to see what others needed, and then to serve them. People were so reticent about what they wanted, eventually no one really knew what they wanted, and in the absence of this knowing, everyone served others. There was a silent language we used to direct our actions. After a time, this process was automatic: observe others, intuit need, then act to satisfy what you thought was wanted. As for resentment and confusion—and desire—you were pretty much on your own.

Then I thought of my brother. What did he want? What did he never say he wanted? Did he know what he wanted? Was not knowing this core thing a vacancy inside himself around which he faltered from this life?

And what did his death teach me I wanted? If he could be alive again, taste huckleberries on this trail, and stand together with a kind friend, what might he want?

A spiderweb tethered to a trunk of pine bellied and flickered in the breeze, a rainbow sheen flowing from one end to the other.

"I want to be honest," I said. "I used to think it was easy. But I didn't know the first thing. If I can be honest, I will be a father. I will be a writer. I want to try to know, to say, to witness what is real."

"So," she said, "you have chosen. Not an easy thing. But you have chosen." She looked far down the trail for a moment. "I have five rules for you then. These last few miles, I've figured out five."

"Rules?"

"First, be a great single parent to your daughter. Someday, you may be with a new partner. But don't wait for that. Be single and a father, and do it well.

"Second, live in a house you love. Don't see your place as a temporary camping spot between your old life and some new life to come. Be who you are, and make your place be about who you are.

"Third, do things with your guy friends. This is a time for friendship. You lost a brother. Seek brotherhood. You know how important that can be.

"Fourth—and this will be a challenge: no significant romantic relationships for a year. You need to sit this out for awhile, let who you are get clearer. Who you are without a wife. Without a girlfriend. Without a brother. Just you."

"Okay," I said, "but what about insignificant romantic relationships?"

She laughed.

"Well, yeah. Here we are, man and woman, yes? Two in one cocoon, yes? But you know what I mean. Don't go into another's life until you have your own."

"And fifth?"

"Was there a fifth?"

"You said five."

"Let me think about it," she said, and turned to take the lead again for the last mile down the trail.

## CRYING CLOTHES

A Nez Perce friend once told me about the custom of the crying clothes at a time of mourning. A year after a death, he said, the family gathers in a circle to pass around the clothing of the one who has died. You take a shirt and say, "This was his shirt. He wore it with honor. He worked in this shirt. He took care of his family. This shirt grew old on his body. But where he is going now, he will not need this anymore. Where he is going, he will not need to wear this shirt." And then, if you cry, said my friend, you cry into that shirt. You wipe your tears into that shirt. You pass that shirt from hand to hand. Everyone says their words, and their tears go into that shirt. And when everyone has spoken, the shirt goes into the fire, and you go on. You put the death behind you.

I told him my brother kept appearing in my dreams. He told me that meant the spirit of my brother was not ready to leave this world. But it was my job, he said, if I loved my brother, to help him go.

I drove east from Portland, turned north at Hood River across the Columbia, and threaded the White Salmon River valley north toward Trout Lake, where my brother had worked one summer for the Forest Service. Beyond Trout Lake is the road to Mount Adams. My parents had my brother's ashes, and my sisters were with them, and they would meet me at Bird Creek Lake at the end of the road. My brother's wife had asked for some of his ashes to scatter in Canada. Somehow it was decided not to respond, but to scatter the ashes ourselves. There was a sharp division between us. Lynne in Canada with the children, Katie and Matt; and we in Oregon with the ashes. Lynne's visit to Portland for the memorial service had become a festival of blaming. She had killed him, I thought—by something I could not see. Why hadn't she told us he had tried? But we had killed him, she may have thought, by our suppression of hard things, our years of pretended good while Bret went deeper into sorrow, isolation, hidden anger. We even went to counseling about it, Lynne and my sisters and I, but the session turned to fury, and she was gone back north.

It seems crazy to me now. That's how it was.

I want to be honest. I want—to be honest. I was already failing. But I knew I was failing. The failure had my attention.

The road from Trout Lake up the mountain is closed in winter, maintained by the Yakama tribe in summer, rocky, crimped turn by turn through the dark forest before climbing out into alpine country and the sun.

I had started very early, arrived at the family camp shortly after dawn, and we took the trail that leads up from the lake toward the open lands called Bird Creek Meadows—lupine, penstemon, fiery paintbrush, huckleberries just beginning to turn crimson, and mountain ash tinged with gold. We were crying. Our father had the box of ashes in his bag. I had never seen him old. He was old on that trail. And mother, she made her birdlike way along the path, cut off from him by the gulf of their lost boy.

My sisters were flowers wilted, dancers crippled, plodding the white dust of the path, a gash of breath, a sob, silence, just the sound of our steps on the rut of the trail.

I can't remember how we decided where. Our father put the box on the ground. One by one, we each took a dusting from the box, and stumbled away, cried, spoke to the spirit of the man, scattered the dust of him over the small alpine trees along the ridge above a tarn. Then the black plastic box was empty, and somehow—I don't remember words—we began to build a cairn where the ridgeline fell away for a deep blue valley to the north. Stone by stone we raised the mound. He was scattered. We were disintegrate. The cairn was our first clumsy effort to put something together—a sorry heap of volcanic stone.

## "IT DOESN'T MATTER WHERE YOU LIVE"

My sister Barb's husband is a realtor, and one morning I called him with an invitation.

"Steve," I said, "in the paper I see the cheapest house west of the river is for sale in my neighborhood. Want to have a look with me?"

"I'll be right over."

We studied the green bungalow I had found, hunched low in its blackberry tangle, windows crooked, roof in need of roofing.

"I would guess that one has no foundation," said Steve. "Looks iffy to me. Let's walk."

Around the corner was a snug house with eyebrow windows peeking from the roof and a big garden.

"You need something like that," he said.

Next door, barely visible through a thicket of holly and hazel, I glimpsed a brown hut far back from the street.

"I'm looking for something more like that," I said. "Just about any house that's cheap, and hidden."

A week later Steve called me. "That hidden house just went on the market," he said. "Sixty-two five. One bedroom."

Later that day we took a look inside. Barely a house—tiny kitchen, living room, midget bathroom, a bedroom with a ceiling that sloped almost too low for me to stand.

"This is it," I said. "Small, cheap, remote." So Steve drew up an offer, and we sent it in.

But the next morning I woke with a feeling of disquiet so heavy, I could not get out of bed: a house—for me? How could that be right? Something I wanted—I the little brother, selfish and blind? I couldn't even keep my brother alive. What comfort did I deserve? A rental on Custer, odd jobs, living alone—isn't that limited life more my size?

I had to talk with someone, get this straight. Parents? No. Sisters? Not this time. As I lay pinned to the bed I realized the one person I wanted to talk with was my brother.

In fifteen minutes I was in the car driving toward Mount Adams. Through Portland, east on I-84, north at Hood River, up the valley to Trout Lake, and onto the Indian road winding through the forest.

My walk up the trail took years. I was younger at the beginning than I was at the end. I had to take off my shoes, feel the cold dust of that place in my bones. I had to cry, see colors through the mist my eyes made. Over the little creek, past the tarn, to the ridge. The cairn of stones. I got down on my hands and knees: there was my brother, crumbs of ash small enough for an ant to carry. I thought of him at Lacey's Tavern, talking about the water cycle. I thought about the crying clothes. I thought about the faces along any street lighting the world with their secret sorrows.

I lay down beside the cairn, closed my eyes, and slept.

What followed might have been a dream, but it was not. Opening my eyes, I looked across the deep blue canyon to the north. Down there, where I couldn't see, my brother's ashes would be carried in the years ahead, to join the milky glacial melt from the mountain to my left. Down there, my brother's wishes would begin to move. Salmon would taste him. The People would find him in their stories. He would travel wise, independent, and far.

I spoke softly to the deep blue below me: "Shall I live in the hidden house? Brother, do I deserve . . . ?"

Across the valley, I saw a light, a flash, a winking glimmer coming in my direction. Dark. Spark. Dark. Spark. I realized it was the gray feathers of a bird flying toward me, folding its wings, unfurling its wings. And out of that pulsing light my brother said, "It doesn't matter where you live. It matters that you live. It matters how you live."

I placed a stone on the cairn of my guardian spirit, thanked my brother, and went home.

# AFTERWORD:
## WHAT CAN WE TRUST BUT MEMORY?

This is a book of questions, a beginning—not a last word, or an end. In spite of everything I can remember or try to puzzle out, my brother will remain a mystery, and his final act an enigma. But there is a consoling optical effect with memory: when certain events get far, they gain focus. Over time, I can see with greater clarity my relation with my brother, who took his life with a gun, and my father's relation with his brother, who took his life with alcohol. I see my brother's children; I see my uncle's children. And there is no simple thing to say. The relation looms forth between my brother's inner life and his outer behavior, between my own silences and my writing. Over time, events become memories, and memories become stories, and in the process we may learn the trick to understand. For it is a trick; it doesn't just happen.

As the old saying goes, life is lived forward but understood backward. "If only I had known . . ." is a futile cry. You don't know until you do, and that takes time—but not marking time. It takes time interrogating silence, facing down darkness, seeking truth. The telling in this book had to be capricious in time, for often former things illuminate later things, but sometimes the present clarifies the past—like sunlight stepping through a forest from east to west, but also glancing back to brighten hidden things that were shadowed at dawn.

Home ground is my brother's ground, and these places keep teaching me: Hood River, Salem, Mount Adams, Eugene, Strawberry Mountain—wherever I go, my brother's places shimmer in their own strange light. My soul has pockets, and into these pockets gather the places and moments that mutter my brother's life, and from this muttering, if I can attend, some clarity may come. He was to have been my guide, the older one, wise counselor. In place of him, his story may be my compass. Like a navigator on the open sea, I have to triangulate with the tools I have: my memory of him, my own life episodes that feel in keeping with his story, and what I am learning with my second wife, Perrin, and our son.

Some of the stories in this book I have told before. The mystery of telling stories from memory, I find, is that they keep revealing new dimensions. The perennial story called "You Can't Eat Beauty," for example, here is a matter of life and death. And the story of my father's assessment of my brother as a saint here carries a dark twist.

As E. O. Wilson says, the honeybees, when they dance, tell each other the oldest story of all: "I want to show you where I found some food." This, too, is my goal—to look back into early times in my family's life, a time flickering with shadows and honey, in order to locate there what will feed us now.

When I began to write this book, I recognized the sheer volume of my memories of my brother—story after story thronged to mind. At the same time, I recognized the uncertainty of memory—detail after detail I could not remember, or might remember wrong. My question at the outset: What can I trust about memory?

As I began to write, though, I also recognized that the recollections I do have of my brother, of my family, and of the historical period spanned by this book—these memories are filled with episodes of severe reticence, denial, and suppression. Painful acts like suicide, and mysterious life dimensions like depression, tend to call forth both indelible memories and a velvet cloak of silence.

As a passage out of silence, memory is the chrysalis of the invisible: a plodding fact goes into the mind, you dither and ponder and dream and write, and a story with rudimentary wings may struggle forth. Memory is an event-based sermon to the self, rooted in secular fact, but wicking the water of spirit up from hiding. The factual details of memory alone may be suspect, but the meanings they sift from the forgotten—these may be the gold we carry still when our treasure is gone. Where sorrow came like a wheeled vessel, and took my brother away (violence, blood, silence), memory and this telling bring him partway back.

Some years after my brother died, I dreamed that all along the linen ribbon winding the body of a mummy is a line of writing—the sequential voice of the person from first utterance to last words. By unwinding this ribbon, according to my dream, by moving sequentially backward in time, you eventually reach the core, which then comes to life.

So, memory cannot be trusted without question, but cannot be suppressed without peril. How can I trust my listening now if I forget that when my brother said he was going away, I thought he meant geographically? If memory has honor, death tunes the ear.

Another danger in such an undertaking, though, is retrospective clarity: because my brother's life ended in suicide, I am tempted to ascribe prophetic meaning to certain early experiences. Is there a connection between his childhood speculation about a gun that said the owner's name, and his own act with a pistol at the age of forty? If my brother had not died by his own hand, that early story would be just another jewel of the childhood imagination. As it stands, I read meaning into early details in light of later events. Is this wrong?

To answer, I take my cue from my brother. He was a historian, and would sift clues from the past, as I would, for the benefit of the living today. I have tried to tell episodes from my brother's life, from our father's life, from my life, and from the life of my son in such a way that readers will be free to draw many of their own conclusions. I have tried to make the parts of the story I remember available for us all in what James McConkey called "the court of memory." In this court, tough moments from the past are called to stand and deliver. As the old man tells Marlow in *Lord Jim*, "In the destructive element immerse." The destructive element is that essential realm where easy explanations won't do. Into this element, I must blunder. And as I blunder, on this journey, in these investigations, I can represent no one finally but myself, on my quest into what none of us can see by daylight.

There is a sense in which my brother's suicide was simply a matter of chemistry, of physical outcome: he was not sleeping, he was on antidepressants that had intensifying side effects when combined with alcohol, and his last afternoon, under severe stress, carrying this paralyzing chemistry, he accepted a beer and, soon after, took his life. But again, chemistry does not explain my brother's long decline into darkness—a decline that I could see in detail only after he was gone. In this, too, memory is the friend of the long truth, if not the short answer. There is a reason I'm writing this story almost a quarter century after the event. They say that suicide is a permanent solution to a temporary problem. But life itself is temporary. So my intent is to tell this history, not of a suicide, but of a life that should not be hidden.

In any forest stand tall trees reaching high for light. Ponderosa, cedar, Douglas fir, sequoia—these, we celebrate: "Avenue of the Giants." But there is also "the understory," that dim tangle of life down low: shrub, fern, vine, spindly young tree snubbed for lack of sun. So, too, in any life there is the understory, the narrative that begs from hiding for light, a glance, a voice. This is the realm of dreams, of stories half-remembered, when a certain trick of light at evening or a chance remark overheard summons from the shadows a story long deferred. I seek to honor the understory of my brother's life, for that understory will not otherwise let me be.

I am pressed by his absence to seek connection. When he was alive, I barely knew about his master's thesis in anthropology: "Harmonious Relations: A Core Cultural Value of the Southern Plateau Indians." Now that he is gone, I read every word, and find his search for pacifism in the garb of study. When I go into the mountains, he is never far. As I step into a sunlit meadow, a voice in my mind says, *I am feeding my brother.* I am tasting for him the colors and flavors of the wild. And at my desk tonight, in place of writing him a letter, I am writing this.

I call this reappearance of my brother "Bret's last trick," a stunning, impossible, recurring, and infinitely precious sleight of his hand.

Could I have saved my brother? Sometimes I think by some deft combination of actions, by turns tender and coercive, I might have bent his destiny. Friends tell me I am wrong. But even if we could not have changed the outcome, my brother did not have to be so alone for so long. The more I consider his life, the more I turn my attention from the final day to the long siege. I see now how I may have sidelined him from the inner circle of my affections. I did not look closely enough at the difficulty he hid from me. If I could not save him then, I may now save some of his stories, and at this distance from his life, deepen our relation. For if there is one thing my brother's story teaches me, it is that the trick of life is harmonious relations, and the key to harmonious relations is talking bravely. This I failed to do then. This I try to do now.

So I have written in this book what the philosopher José Ortega y Gassett called "salvations"—short narratives that seek to apprehend and to save essential stories and discoveries: a moment, a fleeting glimpse, any episodic evidence toward understanding.

By studying my brother's story, I learn that this life is not finally about how long one can be alive in the world, but how to be most alive while here. One way to be most alive is to savor the long view. One of my grandfathers was called to the ministry while working in the fields. The other carried a copy of Poe's "Annabel Lee" in his pocket. These elements of their character remain with me. I carry these men, as I carry my brother. Maybe someday a grandchild of mine, grown old, will tell how I pointed to the wind moving through the grasses when the world was very young. And maybe that old child will give away a copy of this book, the work of two hundred years by then, to a stranger in need. My brother's story will live in that far place. For the work of memoir is to put personal memory in a form that may serve the memories of others.

I remember visiting my sister Barb one night, some years after our brother had died. Our children swirled about us, our mother enjoying the scene, my wife, Perrin, and Barb's husband, Steve, at work in the kitchen. Inside all that, I saw my sister's fingers pick up a card on the dining table, and in her exact gesture I saw my brother's way with finger and thumb. It would be impossible to detail what made his gesture visible, but there it was, unmistakable, and then it was gone. With that gesture, with that hand, in her studio she paints amazing views of the healing world.

Or I watch my sister Kit, at her little ranch in the desert, the stream just there, rolling along, the well, the slough filled with yellow leaves, and the garden, the barn stocked with the amazing artifacts of her art-making. And just at my shoulder, I have our brother gazing with wonder at all she has made.

Our mother, too, carries some of the best of my brother. After I wrote a book about our father, mother wrote her own book to set the record straight. I had described him as a brooding philosopher, she pointed out to me, while she knew him as an affable, constructive person. I'm glad I told my story of him that prompted her, then, to tell her own. And her recollections of my brother are an album, in her own way, of his triumphs and his mysteries.

When I have a chance to visit with my brother's children, Katie and Matt in Canada, I see the best of their father. I see Matt's fine facility with the guitar, his idealism and ability to work hard in pursuit of what he believes. And Katie's wide adventuring, riding her bike across the world, camping, teaching, living with zest. The two of them are my brother striding forth.

There is no way I can tell my brother's story. That would be the work of the many who knew him. Instead, I write my stories of my brother. These are the stories that are mine to tell. And I write these stories for someone I may never meet, a person like you, or someone close to you—a person wondering, struggling, feeling alone in a tough predicament. For that person, all must be told—the good times, bad times, turnings, threats, reprieves—the possibility of an outcome formed of seemingly insufficient materials, but advancing, if we give it time, into survival, and finally blessing.

We are my brother. And also dreams, old songs, places, episodic little movies that scroll through the mind—these, too, are the man. When he was far away, in that first year of college at Grinnell, he wrote home, thanking everyone for their letters, except me. Apparently, I had not been writing him: "I would be interested in hearing about your jobs and school," he wrote, "if you should ever have time to write."

Now I take that time to write. As I write, I realize I have been proven wrong about things I remembered for sure. I can't trust every individual memory to be factually accurate. But I do trust memory itself, the way by writing and reaching, memory plucks and holds from the passing show those moments that best distill what we are about, far beyond what we have been. In writing this book, I thought I would simply remember things, and write them down. Instead, my experience has been this: by beginning to write what I don't understand, I learn how to remember. As I write, scraps of memory gather detail and meaning. As a therapist once told me, little things looked at begin to grow. Memory hidden becomes a fossil; memory spoken or written becomes a lens.

In one of the *Fifty Famous Stories* from our childhood, the Spartan youth, forbidden to have a pet, hid a fox pup inside his cloak. A swaggering superior grilled him about it, but the boy said nothing, did not deny, did not reveal—and all the while the fox cub "gnawed his vitals." I remember those words. Gnawed his life, his manhood, his core being. And since my brother's death, I have seen a quiet contortion on many faces. So it is for anyone who tries to trap a difficult sorrow, to hold it close, to keep hidden the rage of a hard story.

Some around me seem to stop breathing when Bret's name comes up. As a friend said to me, with such grief it's as if you are supposed to hold your breath, and get used to it. It's as if the death means the loving has to stop. But when the courier brings the darkest possible news to MacDuff, and cannot speak hard things, Shakespeare tells us all:

Give sorrow words:
The grief that does not speak
Whispers the o'er-fraught heart
And bids it break.

Give sorrow words. With words, stories spoken, the love, in fact, goes on. My brother kept silent in his pain—and broke. We must not do so.

When my brother died—way back in 1988, and only yesterday—it seemed his life was gone from me, and his death was a huge thing, the suffocating force. In time, gradually, painfully, but surely as I have written, that proportion has been reversed. Now his death is smaller than his life, which keeps growing in my mind and heart. His life is the big thing, his death the fact that dwindles smaller than his spirit looming large. My brother begins to blossom inside my body like a flower opening inside a pool. He has gone there inside, and has become a resident of who I am. I reach out my hand but can't touch him. He is reaching with me, instead, toward something else. Something that calls my attention now.

Since my brother died, in fact, we have never been apart. He is with me every day. Remembering, learning, writing, growing, discovering him again—these have been my own version of the trick by which he reappears. I have to write in order to bring him forth from the shadows. I set out to write the story of how my brother disappeared—from the world, and from my family's conversation—but by writing I find he begins to reappear as a rich dimension in my life. If I did not listen deeply enough to my brother when he was alive, I have been listening since he died. He has become one of my greatest teachers. Bret's life story has given me the choice to grow, or to die, a little at a time. In this process, my brother has been stern and tender, a guide and a warning. Looking back, I see that he was always a little beyond—older, wiser about many things, but also elusive, remote from my reach. Many things he knew, he kept from me, some out of shame, perhaps, and some out of anger and despair, and many out of a certain kind of love. As our father had it, "Why tell what hurts?"

In this book I have been required to tell what hurts. I find the darkest things hurt more when they are not told. The darkest things are still there, battering the interior, but without remedy. Out of love for him, for myself, and for everyone, now I have to let his story go.

# ACKNOWLEDGMENTS

First and greatest honor goes to my brother, Bret, for his example and long companionship in the busy mysteries of this life. I thank you, I listen to you, I learn from you, I reach out to you.

As our father's literary executor, I have direct access to the writings, both public and private, of William Stafford. I am grateful to Doug Erickson, Jeremy Skinner, and Paul Merchant at the William Stafford Archives, Lewis & Clark College, for their ongoing care with these materials, and generous help when requested.

Our mother, Dorothy Hope Stafford, has wondered with me about Bret's amazing life. Likewise my sisters, when they were able, despite deep and continuing grief, have helped me venture into our heritage in order to tell my part.

I thank my niece and nephew, Katie and Matthew Massett Stafford, for putting up with me when I talk and talk a
bout their father. My opportunity now is to welcome them into my life on their own amazing terms.

I would like to thank my students at the Northwest Writing Institute and elsewhere for their acts of witness over many years, by writing about difficult subjects, and their encouragement to me to enter my own difficult realms with a ready pen. I have quoted several of these students in this book and learned courage and ways to adventure in the art of story from many, many others.

Friends from all over have accompanied me for years in puzzling over the memories and questions that form this book. Thanks to all who listened, counseled, and befriended who I am trying to be. And thanks to those who offered particular stories and insights that have helped me see my brother in new ways.

Many people helped me write this book, and some others will tell me I have it wrong. I'm sure I do in some respects—misdirected in emphasis, sometimes wrong in fact. What I set out to do is fill a silence and start a conversation. I welcome correction, but even more I welcome many voices telling their own stories of my brother and of these important matters: passion, pacifism, silence.

I offer my deepest gratitude to my wife, Perrin, and our son, Guthrie, and my daughter, Rosemary, for their unfailing encouragement in this writing project. They have helped me stay the course and find the time to make this book, keeping faith with the notion in our wedding vows to turn silence into words.

I would like to thank Kathleen Holt at *Oregon Humanities Magazine* for permission to reprint, in slightly different form, the essay "Résumé of Failures." Also thanks to the editors of the Lewis & Clark *Chronicle*, who published an earlier version of "Talking Recklessly." I would like to thank the Geography Department at Oregon State University and the library staffs at the University of Victoria and at the University of Oregon for permission to reprint passages from my brother's papers there.

And great good thanks to Barbara Ras, my friend and editor at Trinity University Press, who responded to my first mention of this project with the kind of welcome that made me finally begin to write.

No one but me is responsible for what I have written—right or wrong, saintly or sinful, revealing or resistant—for I am still resistant, often, despite all I can do, to reveal hard things. This is my story of my brother. I believe he has found some peace. And so have I.

**KIM STAFFORD** has taught since 1979 at Lewis and Clark College, where he is the founding director of the Northwest Writing Institute and co-director of the Documentary Studies program. He also serves as the literary executor for the estate of William Stafford. He has worked as an oral historian, letterpress printer, editor, photographer, teacher, and visiting writer in communities and at colleges across the country, and in Italy and Bhutan.

Stafford has published a dozen books of poetry and prose, including *The Muses among Us: Eloquent Listening and Other Pleasures of the Writer's Craft*; *Early Morning: Remembering My Father, William Stafford*; and *Having Everything Right: Essays of Place*. He has received two National Endowment for the Arts creative writing fellowships, the Oregon Governor's Arts Award, and a Western States Book Award. He lives in Portland, Oregon, with his wife and children.